Reading for the Gifted Student

Challenging Activities for the Advanced Learner

Written by **Danielle Denega**

Illustrations by **John Haslam**

An imprint of Sterling Children's Books

FLASH KIDS, STERLING, and the distinctive Sterling logo are registered trademarks of
Sterling Publishing Co., Inc.

Published by Sterling Publishing Co., Inc.
387 Park Avenue South, New York, NY 10016
Text and illustrations © 2005 by Flash Kids
Distributed in Canada by Sterling Publishing
c/o Canadian Manda Group, 165 Dufferin Street
Toronto, Ontario, Canada M6K 3H6
Distributed in the United Kingdom by GMC Distribution Services
Castle Place, 166 High Street, Lewes, East Sussex, England BN7 1XU
Distributed in Australia by Capricorn Link (Australia) Pty. Ltd.
P.O. Box 704, Windsor, NSW 2756, Australia

Sterling ISBN 978-1-4114-3430-1

Manufactured in Canada

Lot #:
4 6 8 10 9 7 5 3
05/12

For information about custom editions, special sales, premium and
corporate purchases, please contact Sterling Special Sales
Department at 800-805-5489 or specialsales@sterlingpublishing.com.

Cover image © Bounce /Getty Images
Cover design and production by Mada Design, Inc.

Whether your student has been identified as gifted and talented or is simply a scholastic overachiever, school-assigned activities may not be challenging enough for him or her. To keep your student engaged in learning, it is important to provide reading activities that quench his or her thirst for information and allow opportunities to exercise critical thinking.

This workbook contains much more than typical reading passages and questions; it does not rely on the assumption that a gifted and talented fourth-grader simply requires fifth-grade work. Instead, the nearly 200 pages of reading passages, comprehension questions, and creative activities are calibrated to match the average reading level, analytical capacity, and subject interest of this specialized group of learners. Specifically, the vocabulary, sentence structure, and length of passages in this grade 4 workbook are set at levels normally appropriate for grades 5 and 6, but the comprehension skills increase in difficulty as the workbook progresses, starting with grade 4 curriculum standards and working through those associated with grade 5. The passages' topics are primarily nonfiction and present concepts, themes, and issues fundamental to all disciplines, including science, social studies, health, and the arts.

Question formats range from multiple choice and short answer to true-or-false, fill-in-the-blank, and much more. Also sprinkled throughout the workbook are creative activities that will encourage your student to write a story or draw a picture. Your student may check his or her work against the answer key near the end of the workbook, or you may wish to review it together, since many questions have numerous possible answers.

Reading, writing, and language skills are essential to any student's academic success. By utilizing this workbook, you are providing your gifted learner an opportunity to seek new challenges and experience learning at an advanced level.

Contents

Plant Power

Plants serve several important purposes for both the environment and humans. First, plants produce food. Plants are the only organisms that can convert the sun's light energy into food. They do this through a process called photosynthesis. Even if you do not eat plants, they are the original source of your food. This is because the animals we sometimes eat, such as chickens and cows, eat plants to survive and grow.

As plants make food, one of the materials they produce is oxygen. Oxygen is a second reason why plants are important. Oxygen makes up part of the air we breathe so it is vital for humans and animals. We can't live without it!

Plants are also important because they are the main habitat for thousands of other organisms. Plants provide shelter and safety for animals. They provide shade, help control air temperature, and protect animals from the wind and weather.

Plants also play a role in creating rich soil. When plants die, their decomposed, or rotted, remains go back into the soil. This makes the soil rich with nutrients, which makes even more plants grow!

Another important role that plants have is providing useful products for humans. In addition to food, plants give us fiber for making cloth. We also use plants to create medicines and burn plants to create heat and energy.

Circle *true* or *false* after each statement about the reading.

1. Plants are the main habitat for thousands of other organisms.   **true   false**

2. Plants are one of many kinds of organisms that can convert
the sun's light energy into food.   **true   false**

3. Plants provide shelter and safety for animals.   **true   false**

4. When plants die, their decomposed remains go back into the soil.   **true   false**

5. Oxygen is not vital for humans and animals to survive.   **true   false**

6. Plants provide useful products for humans.   **true   false**

Plant Parts

Use the descriptions to label the correct parts of the plant on the diagram below.

Leaves: The leaves of a plant are designed to capture sunlight. That is why they are usually broad and flat. This surface area allows them to catch more light. Plants use their leaves to make food through a process called photosynthesis.

Roots: Roots help the plant obtain nutrients from the ground. They act like straws as they suck in minerals to help the plant thrive. Roots anchor a plant in the soil, so that the plant does not tip over or separate from the soil. A plant's roots also store extra food for future use.

Stem: The stem holds the plant upright, the way bones in your body hold you up. The stem also acts like a pipe through which water, nutrients, and food travel throughout the plant, nourishing all its parts. Some plants have flexible stems, such as the stem of a daffodil. Other plants have stiff stems, such as the trunk of a tree.

Flower: The flower is often the pretty part of a plant. But it also has a purpose. Flowers contain a substance called pollen and tiny eggs called ovules. The flower is the reproductive part of a plant, or the part that helps more plants develop.

Seeds: Seeds contain tiny new plants. They are located inside the flower.

Pollination

Pollination is the process by which seeds grow into new plants. Did you know that flowers have male and female parts, like people? This is true, except that each flower has both male and female parts! These parts enable them to reproduce, or create new plants.

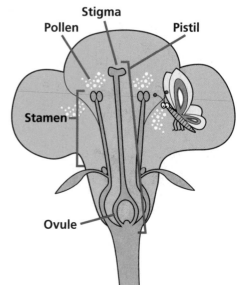

The male parts of a flower are called stamens. Stamens produce a sticky powder called pollen. Flowers also have a female part called the pistil. The top of the pistil is called the stigma. Seeds are made at the base of the pistil, in the ovule.

In order for pollination to occur, pollen must move from a stamen to the stigma. This can happen in several ways. Sometimes the wind blows pollen around and it lands in the right place. At other times, an insect such as a bee or butterfly carries the pollen. While feeding, these insects often rub against the stamens of the flower and get pollen all over their bodies. When they move to another flower to feed, some of the pollen rubs off onto this new flower's stigma. Thus, these insects accidentally cause pollination!

Answer the questions about the reading.

1. What is the definition of *pollination*? _____

_____

2. What are the male parts of a flower called? _____

3. What important material do these parts produce? _____

4. Where are seeds made? _____

5. What must happen in order for pollination to occur? _____

_____

6. What role do insects play in pollination? _____

_____

Fruit or Vegetable?

Have you ever wondered about the difference between a fruit and a vegetable? So have many other people! The answer can be confusing, mostly because people often use the incorrect terms for fruits and vegetables. Foods we often call vegetables, such as tomatoes, are really fruits!

Think of it this way: According to botanists, or scientists who study plants, a fruit is the ripe ovary or ovaries of a flower. The ovary ripens when the ovules inside have been fertilized. Seeds of flowering plants are found inside this ripe ovary, or fruit. Examples of fruits are apples, oranges, grapes, and the ever-confusing tomato.

Vegetable is a term that grocery stores use to refer to all of the edible parts of a plant, such as the roots, stems, and leaves. Examples of root vegetables are carrots and potatoes. Celery, for example, is actually the stem of a plant. And vegetables like lettuce and spinach are the leaves of a plant.

So what does that make a mushroom? Mushrooms are neither fruits nor vegetables. Rather, they are fungi. But that's another story!

Unscramble the words mentioned in the reading.

1. tatoomes _____

2. essed _____

3. blegetave _____

4. bnistsota _____

5. oryva _____

6. otros _____

Fruit Smoothie

PINEAPPLE-ORANGE SMOOTHIE RECIPE

Ingredients:

1 cup orange juice

2 cups pineapple chunks in their own juice, drained

1 banana

$\frac{1}{4}$ cup skim milk

2 Tbsp. honey

4–5 ice cubes

Directions:

1. Place all ingredients in a blender.
2. With the help of an adult, purée until smooth.

Note: Different fruits or juices may be added or substituted.

Use the recipe to answer the questions.

1. How much honey do you need? Underline the amount.

2. How much orange juice is required? Underline the amount.

3. How many ice cubes are necessary? Underline the number.

4. What do you do with all the ingredients in the blender? _____

_____

5. What do you think might happen if you used whole milk instead of skim milk? _____

_____

6. Name one fruit you would add or substitute. _____

Gardening Grace

Grace simply adores gardening. She gardens nearly every single day. Grace loves spending time outdoors in the fresh air. She enjoys digging her hands into the earth. Grace finds joy in watching all of the insects and animals that come to visit her gardens. And most of all, Grace feels extremely proud of her gardens whenever someone sees them or eats something from them.

Grace grows many things in her gardens. On one side of her home, Grace has an herb garden in which she grows basil, rosemary, dill, and thyme. She likes to use these herbs to spice her cooking. Grace also grows fruits and vegetables in a separate garden in her backyard. In that garden, Grace nurtures tomatoes, spinach, carrots, and peppers.

Perhaps Grace's most beautiful garden is the flower garden that adorns her front lawn. Grace has a large variety of flowers, including perennials, which grow back for many years. Pink peonies and roses bloom in the spring. Lilies, begonias, and marigolds brighten the space. Black-eyed Susans and daisies sprout all around. Grace even has many lovely trees on her property, including a Japanese maple and a weeping willow.

Needless to say, Grace's love of gardening pleases both herself and her neighbors. I wonder what Grace will grow in her garden next!

Answer the questions about the story. Write the letter of the answer on the line.

1. How often does Grace garden? _____

    a. once a week

    b. nearly every day

    c. never

2. What does Grace use her herbs for? _____

    a. bathing

    b. decoration

    c. cooking

3. Which of Grace's gardens does the author think is most beautiful? _____

    a. flower garden

    b. herb garden

    c. vegetable garden

4. What does *perennial* mean? _____

    a. a plant that re-grows for several years

    b. a plant that dies at the end of a season

    c. a plant that grows only every five years

Tree Trivia

Trees are the tallest kind of plants. They are woody plants with stems at least 15 feet high when fully grown. Their main stem, called a trunk, is what most clearly distinguishes trees from other plants.

Trees are perennials. Perennials are plants that live for at least three years. However, trees often live for many more years than that. In fact, scientists believe that one specimen of bristlecone pine tree is about 4,600 years old!

Trees exist in a wide variety of sizes. Some trees only reach about 15 feet, while others grow to be hundreds of feet high. One such type of tree is the General Sherman Tree. The General Sherman is a giant sequoia found in California's Sequoia National Park. It reaches the astounding height of 275 feet!

Trees grow all over the world and in all kinds of environments, including the Arctic and the equator. A single tree can grow in a given spot, but oftentimes trees are found in groups called stands. Stands consist of either one species of tree or a mixture of tree species. Stands are often found in forests. Forests are plant communities composed of trees, shrubs, and herbs. In North America, forests usually include just a few species of trees. But in tropical forests, numerous different species of trees can be found. For example, in the rain forests of Brazil in South America, an estimated more than 475 different species could be found within a $2\frac{1}{2}$-mile radius!

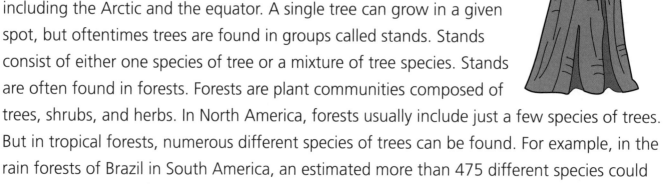

Use what you learned from the reading to fill in the blanks.

1. The tallest types of plants are _____.

2. Trees have a main stem, called a _____.

3. Trees usually grow in groups called _____.

4. _____ are plant communities composed of trees, shrubs, and herbs.

5. The _____ grows to be 275 feet tall.

6. Brazil is located in _____.

Arbor Day

Arbor Day is observed every year to encourage tree planting and care. The national Arbor Day is celebrated on the last Friday of April.

Arbor Day was the idea of a pioneer named J. Sterling Morton. In 1854, Morton moved from Detroit, Michigan, to what was the Nebraska Territory. But when he got there, Morton found that Nebraska was generally a treeless place. Morton loved nature, so he quickly planted many trees and other plants near his new home.

J. Sterling Morton worked for the local newspaper, where he wrote about agriculture and his love of trees. He encouraged others to plant more trees, an idea that excited everyone. Other pioneers also missed the beauty of trees, but they also realized that the Nebraska Territory needed trees for practical reasons, too. Trees were a necessary source of fuel and building material. They would also help block the wind that barreled across the plains and provide shade from the hot summer sun.

Morton became a prominent figure in the local area. In 1872 he attended a meeting of the State Board of Agriculture, where he suggested a tree-planting holiday: Arbor Day! Thus, the first Arbor Day was celebrated on April 10, 1872. Eventually, Arbor Day was made a legal holiday in Nebraska. J. Sterling's birthday, April 22, was selected as the date for its permanent observance in that state.

Number the events in the correct order.

_____ Morton quickly planted many trees and other plants near his new home.

_____ Morton moved from Detroit, Michigan, to what was the Nebraska Territory.

_____ Morton became a prominent figure in the local area.

_____ Arbor Day was made a legal holiday in Nebraska.

_____ Morton found that Nebraska was generally a treeless place.

_____ Morton attended a meeting of the State Board of Agriculture, where he suggested a tree-planting holiday.

Forest Classification

There are several types of forests. They are divided by climate and location.

Type of Forest: Tropical rain forest
Characteristics: Tropical rain forests have high temperatures all year long. They also receive a large amount of rain, which makes them dense and lush. Tropical rain forests are found near the equator.

Type of Forest: Subtropical forest
Characteristics: Subtropical forests are found north and south of tropical rain forests. The trees in subtropical forests have adapted to drier climates that have little to no rainfall.

Type of Forest: Montane forest
Characteristics: Montane forests are also called cloud forests because they receive most of their precipitation from mist or fog. The trees are mainly conifers, or cone-bearing trees. Animals and other plants in these forests have adapted to withstand cold, moist conditions, and strong sunlight.

Type of Forest: Mediterranean forest
Characteristics: Mediterranean forests are found around the coasts of the Mediterranean Sea, California, Chile (in South America), and Western Australia. The growing season in Mediterranean forests is short and almost all their trees are evergreens.

Type of Forest: Coniferous forests
Characteristics: Coniferous forests are located in cold, windy regions near the North and South Poles. Both deciduous hardwoods and conifer trees can be found in coniferous forests. The conifers are evergreens that have adapted to withstand long, dry, bitterly cold conditions.

Type of Forest: Temperate forest

Characteristics: Temperate forests are found in eastern North America, northeastern Asia, and western and eastern Europe. Temperate forests contain a mixture of deciduous and coniferous evergreen trees. Rainfall in these forests is plentiful, and they experience four well-defined seasons.

Match each type of forest to its characteristic.

montane forest   found north and south of tropical rain forests

coniferous forest   short growing season

tropical rain forest   experiences four well-defined seasons

temperate forest   high temperatures all year long

Mediterranean forest   also called cloud forest

subtropical forest   located in cold, windy regions near the North and South Poles

Lance's Legacy

Lance Armstrong is one of the world's most celebrated cyclists. From the time he was thirteen years old, Armstrong competed in cycling events, among other sports. When Armstrong was only a senior in high school, he was asked to train with the U.S. Olympic development team. He competed in the 1992 Olympics as a cyclist, and then turned professional shortly after.

In 1993, Lance Armstrong raced his way to ten cycling titles, including the World Championship. He continued to compete for the next several years, but in 1996,

 Armstrong was diagnosed with cancer. His illness was very serious, possibly fatal. At one point, doctors told Armstrong that he only had a 40% chance of surviving the cancer. But he did survive it. Armstrong was declared cancer-free in February 1997.

After his illness, most people thought Lance Armstrong would never race again. However, Armstrong made a comeback that was nothing short of miraculous. He trained and was race-ready by 1998. Then in 1999, Armstrong became the second American ever to win the most respected cycling event: the Tour de France. And he didn't stop there. Lance Armstrong went on to win the Tour de France three more times in a row!

In addition to his racing achievements, Armstrong is the founder of Livestrong, which is a cancer foundation. He has also written several best-selling books and participated in the New York City Marathon.

Write *fact* or *opinion* after each statement from the reading.

1. In 1999, Armstrong became the second American ever to win the Tour de France.

_____

2. Lance Armstrong is one of the world's most celebrated cyclists. _____

3. When Lance Armstrong was only a senior in high school, he was asked to train with the U.S. Olympic development team. _____

4. In 1996, Armstrong was diagnosed with cancer. _____

5. Armstrong is the founder of Livestrong, which is a cancer foundation. _____

6. Armstrong made a comeback that was nothing short of miraculous. _____

Boxing's Best

Cassius Marcellus Clay, now known as the famous boxer Muhammad Ali, brought a style to the boxing ring that the sport hadn't seen before. He is known as one of history's greatest boxers because of his quick jab and fancy footwork. Ali is famous for his phrase "Float like a butterfly, sting like a bee," which he felt described the way he boxed. He would often declare victory over opponents before the fight had even begun.

Born in Kentucky in 1942, Ali started boxing when he was just twelve, but it did not take long for him to become extremely talented. He fought as an amateur boxer from 1954 through 1960, and won 100 of the 108 matches he fought! By 1960, he had won an Olympic gold medal for light heavyweight boxing. Then, Muhammad Ali turned professional and won his first 19 matches. And in 1964, he won boxing's greatest professional title: the heavyweight championship. Around this time, Ali started practicing the Muslim religion, and changed his name from Cassius Clay to the Muslim name Muhammad Ali.

Ali retired from boxing in 1979, and was soon diagnosed with Parkinson's disease, from which he still suffers. But, before his retirement, Ali became the first man to win the world heavyweight title three times. During his boxing career, he locked in 56 wins, 5 losses, and 37 knockouts. Muhammad Ali was chosen to light the Olympic torch at the 1996 games in Atlanta, Georgia, which was an enormous honor. At the turn of the century, Muhammad Ali was the obvious choice to be named the twentieth century's most important sportsman. And in 2005, Ali was even awarded the Presidential Medal of Freedom.

Answer the questions about the reading.

1. What is Muhammad Ali's birth name? _____

2. When was Muhammad Ali born? _____

3. How old was Muhammad Ali when he started boxing? _____

4. From what disease does Muhammad Ali suffer? _____

5. What is Muhammad Ali's famous phrase? _____

6. How many times did Muhammad Ali win the world heavyweight title? _____

Hank's Homers

Henry, or Hank, Aaron is known as the home run king of baseball and was the first black man to gain this type of fame.

Born on February 5, 1934, in Mobile, Alabama, Aaron began his career in the Negro League, and then became part of the Major League in 1954. During his Major League Baseball career, Aaron spent 23 years playing for the Milwaukee Braves (now the Atlanta Braves) and Milwaukee Brewers. He set many of baseball's most prominent records: runs batted in, extra base hits, total bases, and most years with 30 or more home runs. He is also one of the top five players for career hits and runs.

But perhaps Aaron's most notable achievement was breaking Babe Ruth's home run record. On April 8, 1974, Hank Aaron hit his 715th home run, which broke Ruth's record of 714. This was a momentous event for both baseball and the black community. But, unfortunately, Aaron couldn't enjoy it as much as he should have. He was threatened and bothered by racists who were not happy that a black man had broken Ruth's record.

Until 2007, Aaron also held the record for most career home runs: 755. That was the year when another baseball great, Barry Bonds, finally broke Aaron's amazing feat by hitting his 756th home run.

In 1975, Aaron retired from Major League Baseball. Among the many honors he's been granted, Aaron was elected to the National Baseball Hall of Fame in 1982. He also was awarded the Presidential Medal of Freedom in 2002. Major League Baseball even created an award that honors Hank Aaron, which is named after him and is given annually to the best overall hitter in each league.

Match each year to the event that happened.

1974   Henry (Hank) Aaron was born.

1982   Hank Aaron was awarded the Presidential Medal of Freedom.

2002   Barry Bonds broke Hank Aaron's career home run record.

2007   Hank Aaron started playing for the Major League.

1954   Hank Aaron was elected to the National Baseball Hall of Fame.

1934   Hank Aaron hit his 715th home run.

Brian at Bat

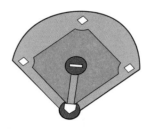

Write your own ending to this story.

It was the bottom of the ninth. Brian stood at home base, with the bat dangling from his right hand. The afternoon sun shone brightly in his eyes. He put his hand to his brow to block the sun and peered around the field. With runners on second and third, the fate of the game fell on Brian's shoulders.

He scraped his cleats against the rusty brown soil and tapped his bat to each foot. He rolled his shoulders backward, and then forward. He stretched his sunburned neck to each side and positioned himself to swing.

_____

_____

_____

_____

_____

_____

_____

_____

_____

Perfect Ten

When you appear on the front of a cereal box, you know that you've made it big. But that was just the icing on the cake for one of the world's best gymnasts, Mary Lou Retton. This tiny powerhouse developed a love for gymnastics as a very young girl. She clearly had talent and needed to train with the best, so Mary Lou Retton sought foremost coach Bela Karolyi.

Retton had a strong, dense frame, making her extremely powerful as she leaped and twisted through the air. Under Karolyi's guidance, Retton won several prominent competitions, including the American Cup and the U.S. Nationals.

But it was the 1984 Olympics that made her a national hero. Mary Lou Retton won a gold medal in the women's all-around, making her the first female gymnast to do this who was not from Eastern Europe. Retton scored a perfect 10—a rarity in gymnastics—during the vault competition, which locked in her all-around gold medal. Plus, she won two silver and two bronze medals in individual and team competitions that year.

Retton continued to succeed, and after winning her third American Cup title, she retired from gymnastics in 1986. In 1997, Mary Lou Retton was granted membership in the International Gymnastics Hall of Fame.

Answer the questions about the reading.

1. Who was Mary Lou Retton's gymnastics coach? _____

2. In what year did Retton compete in the Olympics? _____

3. What was one of her great achievements in that Olympics? _____

_____

4. When did Mary Lou Retton retire? _____

5. What happened to Mary Lou Retton in 1997? _____

_____

Ashe's Achievements

Arthur Ashe is a well-known tennis star, but he also gained attention for promoting racial equality. While in college at the University of California at Los Angeles, Ashe became the first black person ever picked to play on the U.S. Davis Cup Team. Just five years later, he won the men's championship at the 1968 U.S. Open. He was already considered the number-one tennis player in the country!

In 1969, Arthur Ashe turned professional, and shortly thereafter he won the Australian Open. Ashe was the first black man to win the singles competition at Wimbledon, when he defeated Jimmy Connors in 1975. In fact, for more than three decades Ashe was the only black player to win the men's singles at Wimbledon, the U.S. Open, or the Australian Open.

But, Ashe also made great strides for blacks off the tennis court. He was an active member of the anti-apartheid movement. Apartheid was a system of racial unfairness that existed in the country of South Africa. Ashe pushed to change things there, and he was eventually the first black professional tennis player to compete in that country.

Ashe suffered several heart attacks and thus retired from tennis around 1980. Soon after he founded an anti-apartheid organization. Then, in 1992, it was revealed that Arthur Ashe was suffering from the AIDS virus, which he contracted through a blood transfusion. This propelled Ashe to become a spokesperson for AIDS awareness and education. Sadly, Ashe died from complications of AIDS in February 1993.

Complete each sentence about the reading. Circle the letter of the answer.

1. Arthur Ashe attended college at _____.

  a. the University of California at Los Angeles

  b. the University of California at Irvine

  c. the University of Michigan

2. In 1992, it was revealed that Arthur Ashe was suffering from _____.

  a. polio

  b. AIDS

  c. eczema

3. Arthur Ashe was the first black man to win the singles competition at _____.

  a. the U.S. Open

  b. the Australian Open

  c. Wimbledon

4. Arthur Ashe turned professional in the year _____.

  a. 1999

  b. 1996

  c. 1969

Golf's Tiger

Some might say that Tiger Woods was born with a golf club in his hand. It's true that he did start playing golf at a very young age. By the time he was only eleven years old, Tiger Woods had won 33 junior golf tournaments.

In 1996, Woods became a professional golfer, playing in Professional Golf Association (PGA) tours and winning with amazing frequency. One of his most significant wins was at the 1997 U.S. Masters. At the age of 21—a baby in the world of golf—Woods shot a record score of 270. This made Woods both the youngest player and the first player of African descent to win that tournament.

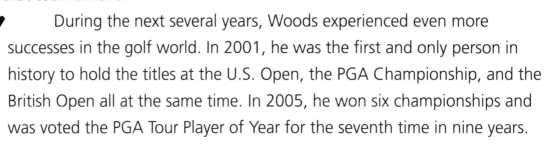

During the next several years, Woods experienced even more successes in the golf world. In 2001, he was the first and only person in history to hold the titles at the U.S. Open, the PGA Championship, and the British Open all at the same time. In 2005, he won six championships and was voted the PGA Tour Player of Year for the seventh time in nine years.

Sadly, in 2006, Woods's father passed away. His father had taught Woods to play golf, so it was a great loss for the golf champ. But, Woods was still able to keep his head in the game, winning both the PGA Championship and the British Open that year. His success has drawn people of all backgrounds to the sport of golf. He is known for his intensity on the course, playing a reserved, focused game, and for his nearly perfect swing.

Answer the questions about the reading.

1. When did Tiger Woods start playing golf? _____

2. When did Tiger Woods become a professional golfer? _____

3. When did Tiger Woods's father pass away? _____

4. When did Tiger Woods become both the youngest player and the first player of African descent to win the U.S. Masters? _____

5. When did Tiger Woods become the first and only person in history to hold the titles at the U.S. Open, the PGA Championship, and the British Open all at the same time? _____

Blair Beats the Best

To say that Bonnie Blair can skate quickly is a vast understatement. At the age of two, Bonnie Blair first stood up on skates, and it was love at first glide. By the time she was four years old, she was already winning races!

Bonnie Blair joined the national speed skating team after she graduated from high school. By the age of 19, she was skating her way into history as an Olympic athlete. In the 1984 Winter Olympics, Blair finished eighth in the 500-meter speed skating sprint, which was a promising start. Then, at the 1988 Winter Games, Blair took home the gold medal. When she won the 500-meter sprint, she set a world record and captured the first of many gold medals.

Continuing her winning streak, Bonnie Blair won the gold medals for both the 500-meter and 1,000-meter races at the 1992 Olympics, and then did it all again at the 1994 Games. Blair had won an astounding five gold Olympic medals and was the first American woman to do so. She was also the first male or female American to win gold medals in the same event in three Olympics in a row.

Despite her Olympic achievements, Blair was still determined to continue making history. She wanted more than gold: Blair wanted to be the fastest female speed skater in history. And that's just what she became. In 1994, she beat the world record in the 500-meter. Then, before her retirement in 1995, she beat her own record!

Bonnie Blair's low crouch and long glide secured her place as one of the world's best athletes. She is still the most awarded woman in Olympic history, and she was elected to the Olympic Hall of Fame in 2004.

Unscramble the words mentioned in the reading.

1. teskas　　　＿＿＿＿＿＿＿＿＿＿＿＿＿＿＿＿＿＿＿

2. eespd stinkag　＿＿＿＿＿＿＿＿＿＿＿＿＿＿＿＿＿＿＿

3. wlord corerd　＿＿＿＿＿＿＿＿＿＿＿＿＿＿＿＿＿＿＿

4. lyoicmps　　＿＿＿＿＿＿＿＿＿＿＿＿＿＿＿＿＿＿＿

5. gldo　　　　＿＿＿＿＿＿＿＿＿＿＿＿＿＿＿＿＿＿＿

6. idgle　　　　＿＿＿＿＿＿＿＿＿＿＿＿＿＿＿＿＿＿＿

Soccer Sam

Sam shook out her long, muscular legs to loosen her muscles. She stretched her socks up over her shinguards and tucked her red-and-white jersey into her shorts. Sam snapped a clip in her short brown hair. She rubbed her cold hands together, clapped to get herself ready, and ran onto the field. She took her place at center midfield, and she jogged in place to stay warm. She watched as her teammates took their positions.

The other team set themselves up on the other half of the field. Sam eyed them all suspiciously. To her, each and every one was a possible threat to her taking home the Section A title. She gave the longest, hardest look to the opponent's star player, Jessica, who was a small, stocky, blond girl even faster than herself.

Sam had faced this team earlier in the season, and her team beat them with relative ease. But then Jessica had been injured with a sprained ankle and wasn't able to play. Sam heard that Jessica had gone through physical rehabilitation with the vengeance of a lion and was playing at peak capacity again.

As a midfielder, Sam was a playmaker, but in this game, she would also be marking Jessica. "Don't let her get past our midfield line, Sam," the coach had stressed. "Once she's got possession, she's nearly unstoppable. But, if she does get the ball, you're the one to stop her, got it?" Sam had nodded, taking on this responsibility with great seriousness.

The referee set the ball on the center field line, backed away, nodded to each striker, and sounded his metal whistle. Game on!

Answer the questions about the story.

1. What is the setting of this story? _____

2. Who is the main character, or heroine, of this story? _____

3. How do you think Sam might be feeling in this story? _____

_____

4. Describe Sam's physical appearance. _____

5. Describe Jessica's physical appearance. _____

Yankee Clipper

Joe DiMaggio had many nicknames, including Joltin' Joe and the Yankee Clipper. He was one of baseball's most graceful and prominent players from the very beginning of his career. DiMaggio signed with the New York Yankees in 1936, and he remained a Yankee outfielder throughout his baseball career.

In his first four seasons as a Yankee, DiMaggio helped the Yankees secure the World Series Championship every year. In 1939, he was named the American League's Most Valuable Player (MVP), a success he would repeat in 1941 and 1947.

Joe DiMaggio became especially famous for an amazing hitting streak in the 1941 season, during which the Clipper got a hit at least once per game for 56 games in a row. And once again that year, DiMaggio and the Yankees won the World Series.

His career statistics were generally amazing: DiMaggio hit 361 lifetime home runs and posted a career batting average of .325. He was elected to the National Baseball Hall of Fame in 1955. And to forever honor Joe DiMaggio, the Yankees retired his uniform number, so that no other Yankee would ever wear Joltin' Joe's #5 on his back.

Use the clues to complete the crossword puzzle about the reading.

Across

1. one of Joe DiMaggio's nicknames

2. Joe DiMaggio's position

3. the team Joe DiMaggio played for

Down

4. Joe DiMaggio's number

5. another of Joe DiMaggio's nicknames

6. Joe DiMaggio was named this in 1939, 1941, and 1947

Tennis King

Billie Jean (Moffit) King was born on November 22, 1943, in Long Beach, California. She learned to play tennis on the public courts near her home, and by the age of 18 she had already won the doubles title at Wimbledon! That was King's first time at Wimbledon, and she and her pairs partner Karen Hantze Susman gained a lot of attention for being tennis players on the rise.

But that is only a small mention in the list of Billie Jean King's accomplishments. She later won 19 more Wimbledon titles—a record. She also won 13 U.S. titles, 4 French titles, and 2 Australian titles. But King felt that, as a female player, she was being overlooked. So she fought for equal prize money for men and women and started focusing on that goal. In 1971, King became the first female athlete to win more than $100,000 for competing.

During her campaign for equality of the sexes in tennis, King played a now-famous match against a male tennis player named Bobby Riggs. Riggs claimed that female tennis players were simply not as good as male players. So, they battled it out. King walked away as the winner, beating Riggs 6-4, 6-3, and 6-3 while an audience of 50 million people watched.

In the early 1970s, Billie Jean King founded the Women's Tennis Association to promote women's tennis and continue to fight for more prize money for female players. King's last major tennis competition was at Wimbledon in 1983. She was elected to the International Tennis Hall of Fame in 1987.

Use what you learned from the reading to fill in the blanks.

1. By the age of 18, Billie Jean King had won the doubles title at _____.

2. She later won _____ more Wimbledon titles.

3. In 1971, King became the first _____
to win more than $100,000 for competing.

4. In 1987, she was elected to the _____.

5. Billie Jean (Moffit) King was born in _____.

6. King played a now-famous match against a male tennis player named

_____.

Wendy's Win

Write a story about what you think has happened. Use the title to guide you.

_____

_____

_____

_____

_____

_____

_____

_____

_____

_____

_____

_____

_____

Kareem Abdul-Jabbar

Before Kareem Abdul-Jabbar became a basketball legend famous for his "skyhook" jump shot, he was a shockingly tall teenager named Lew Alcindor. During high school, he was an All-American player three times, which helped him gain a scholarship to the University of California at Los Angeles. While at UCLA, he was one of the country's top college players. He was even named the National Collegiate Athletic Association Tournament's Most Outstanding Player. Around this time, he became a Muslim, and eventually changed his birth name to a Muslim one: Kareem Abdul-Jabbar.

Abdul-Jabbar then played in the professional league, or the NBA, in 1969 for the Milwaukee Bucks. He played center with grace and agility, which did not go unnoticed. He quickly proved himself as a star, and was named Rookie of the Year in 1970. In the following year, the Bucks won the NBA championship, and Abdul-Jabbar was named Most Valuable Player in the league that year. But that was just the first of his many successes.

By 1975, Abdul-Jabbar was playing for the Los Angeles Lakers, helping them win six NBA championships. He was named the league's MVP five more times—a league record. Ten years later, he was named the Sports Illustrated Sportsman of the Year.

By the time Abdul-Jabbar retired in 1989, he had become a legend. He was the NBA's all-time leading scorer with 38,387 points, the leading shot-blocker with 3,189 blocks, and the first NBA player to play for twenty seasons. He had also played more game minutes than any other player in the NBA.

Answer the questions about the reading.

1. What was Kareem Abdul-Jabbar's jump shot called? _____

2. Where did Kareem Abdul-Jabbar attend college? _____

3. What was the first NBA team that Kareem Abdul-Jabbar played for?

_____

4. How many points did Abdul-Jabbar score during his career with the NBA? _____

5. How many times in total was Kareem Abdul-Jabbar named NBA MVP? _____

The Commonwealth

The Commonwealth of Virginia has a rich history. Here are just a few of its fun facts

Nickname: The Old Dominion

Founded: May 13, 1607, at Jamestown

Date Joined the Union: June 25, 1788

Capitals: Richmond (since 1780);
Williamsburg (1699-1780);
Jamestown (1607-1699)

Population: 7,078,515

Area: 40,767 square miles

Flag: The flag of Virginia contains the state seal in a field of blue. It was first used in the 1830s but not officially adopted until 1930.

Official State Emblems

Beverage: Milk

Bird: Cardinal

Boat: Chesapeake Bay Deadrise

Dog: Foxhound

Flower or Tree: Dogwood

Folk Dance: Square Dancing

Insect: Tiger Swallowtail Butterfly

Shell: Oyster

Find six Virginia-related words in the word puzzle below.

C	F	O	X	H	O	U	N	D	F	B	C	V
R	V	A	Q	E	I	O	A	O	U	D	O	Q
J	A	M	E	S	T	O	W	N	F	T	M	A
R	S	Z	O	I	E	N	I	B	E	Z	M	I
S	U	V	D	V	D	V	O	C	V	U	O	Q
T	A	N	Q	E	O	C	S	I	U	B	N	R
E	C	C	A	O	G	A	T	S	F	E	W	E
B	E	F	O	U	W	F	U	E	L	D	E	V
R	I	C	H	M	O	N	D	I	S	T	A	N
D	Y	Q	B	W	O	V	J	Q	M	I	L	K
D	C	G	Z	A	D	Z	O	U	T	Z	T	A
B	E	R	W	A	E	V	O	E	S	N	H	V

Jefferson's Monticello

The third president of the United States, Thomas Jefferson, dreamed of creating a home for himself in central Virginia. When he was twenty-one years old, Jefferson picked out the site for such a house on the land that was part of his father's estate. He named it *Monticello*, which means "little mountain" in Italian.

Jefferson designed Monticello himself, and, beginning when he was 25, built his 11,000-square-foot home on an enormous hill near Charlottesville, Virginia. The grounds contained fruit and vegetable gardens, groves of trees, and many outhouses for the people who worked the plantation. The location of his home allowed him spectacular views of the mountains.

However, building Monticello on a mountain was not a practical decision. Many tons of stone and timber had to be transported uphill, and there were no large trucks or cranes around back then! Also, there was not enough water in the wells for all the people, animals, and plants on top of the hill, so additional water had to be brought in.

Jefferson took great efforts to decorate his beloved property and home. When Jefferson was the Minister to France, he collected nearly one hundred crates full of furniture and art for the interior of the home. He also collected fruit trees from France and brought them home with him.

Because of the ongoing construction of Monticello, life there was not exactly comfortable for its inhabitants. Jefferson's wife, Martha, lived there until her death. During her lifetime, the house had never been finished. In all, Jefferson spent forty years designing it, building it, tearing it apart, redesigning it, and finally putting it all back together. It was his home for the last 56 years of his life.

Despite the many challenges and discomforts associated with Monticello, Jefferson loved his home and its grounds. Nothing like Monticello had ever been built in colonial America. Jefferson is famously quoted as saying of his home, "I am as happy no where else and in no other society, and all my wishes end, where I hope my days will end, at Monticello."

Answer the questions about the reading.

1. Where is Monticello located? _____

2. How old was Jefferson when construction began on Monticello? _____

3. What does *Monticello* mean in Italian? _____

4. How long was Monticello under construction? _____

5. How long did Jefferson live at Monticello? _____

6. What is the approximate square footage of Monticello? _____

7. Why was Monticello's mountain location impractical? _____

_____

_____

8. From where did Jefferson collect much of the furniture and artwork for Monticello?

_____

Presidential Place

Virginia is known as "the mother of presidents" because eight U.S. presidents were born there.

President: George Washington
Lifespan: 1732–1799
Presidency: 1789–1797
President Number: 1
Born in: Westmoreland County, Virginia
Burial: Mount Vernon, Virginia
Known for: setting precedent for all presidents to come

President: Thomas Jefferson
Lifespan: 1743–1826
Presidency: 1801–1809
President Number: 3
Born in: Albermarle County, Virginia
Burial: Monticello, Virginia
Known for: acquiring the Louisiana Territory

President: James Madison
Lifespan: 1751–1836
Presidency: 1809–1817
President Number: 4
Born in: Port Conway, Virginia
Burial: Madison Family Cemetery, Montpelier, Virginia
Known for: being the Father of the Constitution

President: James Monroe
Lifespan: 1758–1831
Presidency: 1817–1825
President Number: 5
Born in: Westmoreland County, Virginia
Burial: Hollywood Cemetery, Virginia
Known for: stating the Monroe Doctrine

President: William Henry Harrison
Lifespan: 1773–1841
Presidency: 1841
President Number: 9
Born in: Charles City County, Virginia
Burial: William Henry Harrison State Park, North Bend, Ohio
Known for: being the first president to die in office

President: John Tyler
Lifespan: 1790–1862
Presidency: 1841–1845
President Number: 10
Born in: Greenway, Virginia
Burial: Hollywood Cemetery, Virginia
Known for: adding Texas to the country

President: Zachary Taylor
Lifespan: 1784–1850
Presidency: 1849–1850
President Number: 12
Born in: Barboursville, Virginia
Burial: Zachary Taylor National Cemetery, near Louisville, Kentucky
Known for: being the first career soldier to become president

President: Woodrow Wilson
Lifespan: 1856–1924
Presidency: 1913–1921
President Number: 28
Born in: Staunton, Virginia
Burial: National Cathedral, Washington, D.C.
Known for: being the first president to make a radio broadcast

Answer the questions about the presidents.

1. Which president is buried in North Bend, Ohio? _____

2. How many presidents were born in Virginia? _____

3. What is Woodrow Wilson known for? _____

_____

4. Where was Zachary Taylor born? _____

5. Who was the ninth president? _____

6. Where is George Washington buried? _____

7. Which president lived from 1743 to 1826? _____

8. Who was president between 1841 and 1845? _____

GREENWAY

BARBOURSVILLE

PORT CONWAY

STAUNTON

WESTMORELAND COUNTY

ALBERMARLE COUNTY

CHARLES CITY COUNTY

VIRGINIA

Jamestown Settlement

A little more than four hundred years ago, ships full of colonists and sailors left England to establish the first permanent English colony in the New World. In May 1607, the ships arrived at a pear-shaped peninsula in what is now the state of Virginia. The settlers called their colony James Fort, and then James Towne, both in honor of James I, the King of England.

The soil and climate in Virginia seemed perfect for a new settlement. But the early years in Jamestown proved very challenging. Nearly half of the settlers died due to poor choices and management of resources. The colonists built a triangle-shaped fort along the river to protect themselves from the Powhatan, the Native Americans already living there. But there were still quarrels between the settlers and the Powhatan, and even more settlers were killed. Furthermore, a fire ravaged the fort in 1608.

As if life were not bleak enough for the Jamestown settlers, even more of them died from famine and disease in the winter of 1609 to 1610. But the following June, more settlers and additional supplies arrived, which encouraged the existing settlers to endure.

In 1612, life started to improve when the settlers began growing tobacco. It was a good business and the colony prospered, becoming the capital of Virginia for a while. In 1619, the first representative assembly in America was held here.

But Jamestown continued to be attacked frequently by Native Americans. During the next several decades, hundreds more colonists were killed. And in 1676, a group of angry colonists rebelled against the rule of Virginia Governor William Berkeley. Afterward Jamestown was burned down by the group and the colony was eventually deserted.

Write *true* or *false* after each statement about the reading.

1. Jamestown was located in what is now the state of North Carolina. _____

2. Jamestown was burned down by William Berkeley. _____

3. The Native Americans near Jamestown killed many of the settlers there. _____

4. Jamestown began to prosper when the settlers grew cotton. _____

5. Many Jamestown settlers died from famine and disease in the winter of 1609 to 1610.

_____

Chief Powhatan

The Powhatan confederacy was a group of Native American Algonquian tribes that occupied what is now the state of Virginia. When the British first settled there in 1607, they had many encounters with these Native Americans.

A man named Powhatan led the Powhatan confederacy. He was their chief, and he was also called Wahunsonacock or Wahunsenacawh. Powhatan had inherited an empire of six tribes from his father, and he was a proud and respected leader who ruled most of the Tidewater area of Virginia. He also brought approximately two dozen additional tribes into the empire.

When the British landed in the New World and settled in Jamestown, Virginia, they began taking over lands that belonged to Powhatan and his people. This spurred the conflicts between the Powhatan and the settlers. Many settlers were kidnapped and held by the Powhatan during their battles with the native people.

In response, a settler named Captain Samuel Argall kidnapped Powhatan's daughter Pocahontas. Argall hoped that holding the girl hostage would persuade Powhatan to return some of the kidnapped settlers. But their plan did not work. Powhatan let his daughter stay with the settlers, asking only that they treat her well. Pocahontas was held by the settlers until she married one of them: John Rolfe. This marriage marked the beginning of a brief period of peace between the colonists and the Powhatan people.

Powhatan died in April 1618 and was succeeded by his brother Opechancanough.

Answer the questions about the reading.

1. What was the Powhatan confederacy? _____

_____

2. Where did the Powhatan live? _____

3. Who was the leader of the Powhatan? _____

4. Why did Powhatan argue with the Jamestown settlers? _____

_____

5. Who was Pocahontas? _____

6. Who succeeded Powhatan? _____

Pocahontas

Pocahontas was the daughter of Chief Powhatan, the powerful leader of the Powhatan confederacy, a Native American group. *Pocahontas* was actually the girl's nickname, meaning "Little Wanton," which is a playful child. Her real name was Matoaka, and historians think that she was born in 1597.

Pocahontas has become famous because of a story about her involvement with the British settlers. The legend claims that John Smith was captured by the Powhatan people. They were about to execute Smith when little Pocahontas laid her arms and head upon Smith's body to protect him. Chief Powhatan followed his daughter's wishes and spared Smith's life.

Regardless of the legend, Pocahontas did become friendly with some of the settlers of Jamestown and tried to promote peace between the Powhatans and the English colonists. But the conflicts continued and eventually the colonists kidnapped Pocahontas. Pocahontas stayed with the colonists and later fell in love with and married one, named John Rolfe. Pocahontas had converted to Christianity and changed her name to Rebecca Rolfe. The marriage created a few years of peace between the Powhatan people and the Jamestown settlers. The couple even had a son together.

But sadly, Pocahontas died only a few years later. Her funeral was held on March 21, 1617—she was only about twenty. She is immortalized today by the legend of herself and John Smith.

Use the names from the word bank to fill in the blanks.

> Matoaka   John Rolfe   Powhatan   John Smith   Jamestown

1. Pocahontas was the daughter of Chief _____, the powerful leader of the Powhatan confederacy.

2. Her real name was _____.

3. According to legend, Pocahontas saved the life of _____.

4. Pocahontas married a man named _____.

5. Pocahontas was friendly with some of the settlers of _____.

Wolf in Wool

Write your own ending to this fable.

There once was a wolf that loved the taste of sheep. But the sheep nearby were well protected by a shepherd and his dogs. The wolf wanted nothing more than to eat the sheep, but he was constantly being shooed away.

One day, the wolf found the skin of a sheep. The wolf realized that if it wore the sheep's skin, it would look like a sheep from a distance. The shepherd and his dogs would think the wolf was one of the sheep! The wolf would be able to sneak up on a flock of sheep and steal a lamb for its supper.

So the wolf pulled the sheep's skin over itself and crept down into the flock of sheep.

_____

_____

_____

_____

_____

_____

_____

_____

_____

Get Your Zs

Allowing yourself enough restful sleep is one of the best things you can do for your health. Sleeping is as vital as eating healthily and exercising. Sleep gives you the energy to get through your day. It helps you pay attention in school, perform a sport, dance, or play an instrument to the best of your ability.

 Studies also show that sleep improves memory because, while you sleep, your body is actually storing memories. Being deprived of sleep makes you feel tired (of course!), groggy, cranky, and forgetful, and impairs your movements. Basically, sleep recharges your body so that you can continue to function the next day. Sleep scientists are not exactly sure how and why the body uses sleep time to recharge. Regardless, they all agree that sleep is a necessity.

Young people between the ages of 7 and 11 usually need about 9 hours of sleep, if not more. Kids need more sleep than adults for a simple reason: you are more active. Your body is busy growing and changing, and you are often playing sports and doing other demanding activities. However, each person does require a different amount of sleep.

Your sister might prefer to sleep for 10 hours, but you only need to sleep for $8\frac{1}{2}$ hours. If you always wake up feeling refreshed, and without an alarm, then you are likely getting the appropriate amount of sleep for your body. That doesn't mean that you have to be hopping out of bed and singing! But if you can't shake off morning grogginess fairly quickly, you need to consider getting to bed earlier. Remember, your body thrives on it!

Answer the questions about the reading. Write the letter of the answer on the line.

1. What do you think *thrive* in paragraph 4 means? _____

    a. to diminish or reduce

    b. to grow vigorously

    c. to die out

2. What do you think *vital* in paragraph 1 means? _____

    a. necessary

    b. insignificant

    c. unimportant

3. What do you think *impairs* in paragraph 2 means? _____

    a. damages or makes worse

    b. fixes

    c. heals

4. What do you think *deprived* in paragraph 2 means? _____

    a. borrowing

    b. lacking

    c. offering

Good Sleep

Many people face difficulty in falling or staying asleep at night. But there are ways to encourage a good night's rest.

Keep It Cool: Studies show that we sleep better in a cool place. So try to make your bedroom about 68° Fahrenheit when you go to sleep.

Make It Dark: Light tells your brain that it is time to be awake. Buy light-reducing shades or blinds and turn your glowing alarm clock away from you. Also turn off any other sources of light, such as bedside lamps, televisions, and computers.

Keep It Regular: Staying on the same sleep schedule is a guaranteed way to maintain good sleep patterns. Hit the sack at the same time, and wake up at the same time, even on weekends.

Avoid Caffeine: Caffeine is a substance found in coffee, tea, soda, chocolate, and many other foods and drinks. Caffeine wakes the body up. That's why adults drink coffee in the morning. But caffeinating your body late in the day can keep you awake at night, even if you go to bed hours later.

Train Your Brain: Don't do anything in your bed but sleep. That means no watching television, using the computer, talking on the phone, or playing video games in your bed. Your brain learns that bed equals sleep, which will help you fall asleep much faster.

Answer the questions about the reading.

1. Why should your bedroom be cool at night? _____

_____

2. Why should you avoid caffeine late in the day? _____

3. What time should you wake up on weekends? _____

4. Why should you not watch television in bed? _____

_____

Wake Up, Susie

Susie is not a morning person. Every day, Susie's mom comes into her room, singing to wake Susie for school, but Susie just grumbles and rolls over again. In the car, Susie falls back asleep as soon as it pulls out of the driveway!

One morning, Susie's mom told her, "I swear, little Susie, I think you could sleep through a circus parading through your room." Susie mumbled something and continued eating her cereal in silence. It was morning, after all.

The following morning, when her mom opened Susie's bedroom door to wake her, her jaw fell open. Susie's mom witnessed a scene she could barely imagine. Inside Susie's room was a full-blown circus. There was a ringleader, a lion tamer corralling two enormous lions, three African elephants, six monkeys swinging from the chandelier, and four clowns hopping out of their car.

The lion licked Susie's nose. Susie rubbed it and slept on. The ringleader tapped Susie on the shoulder. One of the monkeys jumped up and down on Susie's bed. A clown blew his squeaky horn in Susie's ear. But Susie continued to sleep.

Finally, an elephant showered Susie with water from his trunk. Susie finally sat up in bed, mumbling, "You could have just sung to me, Mom!" Susie's mother stepped out and closed the door again. At least she was awake!

Could it have happened in reality? Write *R* or *I* next to each sentence
from the story to tell whether it could be real or only imaginary.

1. _____ Susie eats her cereal in silence.

2. _____ A clown blew his squeaky horn in Susie's ear. But Susie continued to sleep.

3. _____ A circus magically appears in Susie's bedroom.

4. _____ Susie's mom enters her room to wake Susie for school, but Susie just grumbles and rolls over again.

5. _____ In the car, Susie falls asleep as soon as it pulls out of the driveway.

Sleep Stages

When you go to sleep at night, your brain rests, along with your body, right? That is not the case at all! At night, your brain is just as active as it is when you are awake during the day.

In the first two stages of a 90-minute sleep cycle, you are in a light sleep. Stage 1 sleep isn't all that different from being awake and very relaxed. In fact, many people who are awakened while in the first stage of sleep don't even realize that they fell asleep. When you are in stage 1 or 2 of sleep, it's easy for you to be awakened.

In stages 3 and 4 of a sleep cycle, you are in a much deeper sleep. Your body is very relaxed. It is so relaxed that your heart rate and breathing slow down a lot. If you are awakened while in stage 3 or 4 of a sleep cycle, you will likely feel quite groggy and confused. If you are in stage 3 or 4, someone could be shaking you or an alarm clock could be sounding, but your body would need a while to recognize these enough for you to wake.

Stage 5 of a sleep cycle is known as the REM stage. REM stands for Rapid Eye Movement. Although your eyes are closed while sleeping, under your lids they move around during this stage of sleep. This is often the stage in which you dream.

After a few minutes of REM sleep, the sleep cycle starts over again. You fall back into a stage 1 sleep and move through the pattern over the following 90 minutes.

Answer the questions about the reading.

1. How long is a sleep cycle? _____

2. How many stages are there in a sleep cycle? _____

3. What is the fifth stage of sleep called? _____

4. What often happens in the fifth stage of sleep? _____

5. If a person is awakened from stage 3 or 4, how might he or she feel? _____

_____

6. What is stage 1 sleep similar to? _____

Dream a Little Dream

Dreams are one of the great mysteries of life. Believe it or not, scientists still are not sure exactly why we dream. They do know that humans spend more than two hours of each night dreaming. When you dream, you are in a stage of sleep called REM, or Rapid Eye Movement. REM sleep lasts from five to thirty minutes, and it occurs approximately every 90 minutes. This means you have about five dreams each night.

After observing infants sleeping during REM, scientists in the 1950s began to think that there was even more going on in our bodies than they thought. They began to study sleep and dreaming more deeply and quickly realized that the strange, illogical experiences we call dreams almost always occur during REM sleep.

The famous psychologist Sigmund Freud believed that we dream about silly things so that we don't actually do silly things in our waking hours. New ideas about dreams suggest that they enable us to place certain things into our long-term memories and erase the

memories we don't need. Sometimes this process is so scattered that our dreams don't make sense to us when we think about them later.

Other scientists believe that dreams are the brain's way of trying to make sense of random signals it receives during REM sleep. The brain could be attempting to interpret these signals, which creates a "story." In order for the body not to carry out the "story" or dream, the brain sends signals to the muscles to keep them from acting out your dreams. This causes a temporary paralysis of the arms and legs. If something interferes with this paralysis, people will begin to act out their dreams, by sleepwalking, sleep talking, or flailing around. People can even injure themselves this way!

Unscramble the words mentioned in the reading.

1. adrem   _____

2. alysipars   _____

3. rdpai eey moentvem   _____

4. eepalwkinslg   _____

5. siundgm refud   _____

6. bnrai   _____

Strangest Dream

As you read the story, fill in each blank with any word from
the correct part of speech. Have fun!

Last night I had a _____ dream. I had turned

VERB

_____ and grew a long _____.

COLOR   PART OF THE BODY

I learned to _____ like a _____, and

VERB   ANIMAL

then I met _____ and we _____

CELEBRITY   VERB (PAST TENSE)

together. Next, we traveled to _____ , where I showed

PLACE

my _____ to _____ , who said,

NOUN   PERSON IN ROOM

"_____ ! That's one

EXCLAMATION

_____ -looking _____!"

ADJECTIVE   NOUN

Then, the dream got truly _____ because I

ADJECTIVE

_____ had to swim to _____ ! But,

ADVERB   COUNTRY

it was okay because I had my _____ with me. Never

NOUN

leave _____ without it!

PLACE

Sun Safety

 The ultraviolet, or UV, rays of the sun are extremely damaging to your health. Sun exposure leads to eye damage and skin cancer, in addition to blistering sunburns and wrinkles on your skin. But there are numerous ways to protect yourself from the sun.

One way to shield your skin from the sun's UV rays is to cover your skin with clothing. Opaque cloth provides better protection. You should also cover your head with a wide-brimmed hat to block your scalp, face, and neck from the sun. The sun can be very damaging to your eyes, too, so wear sunglasses that block UV rays. When the temperature is just too hot for extra clothing, sunscreen becomes vital.

Sunscreens are lotions containing chemicals that protect your skin from UV damage. The container is marked with SPF, which stands for Sun Protection Factor. The higher the SPF number, the longer you can stay in the sun while wearing it. Sunscreen should be applied liberally. That means you should generously coat every inch of your skin with lotion and rub it in well. You should apply sunscreen thirty minutes prior to sun exposure because your skin needs time to absorb the lotion first.

Sunscreen should also be applied several times during the course of the day, especially if you have been in water or sweating. The benefits of sunscreen wear off after it has been on for a few hours. Many sunscreens claim to be waterproof or sweat proof, but you should ensure that you are protected, so you should still reapply.

If you don't have proper clothing or sunscreen, you should simply stay out of the sun, especially during its peak hours. The rays of the sun are strongest, and therefore most damaging, between 10 AM and 2 PM.

Answer the questions about the reading.

1. What does UV stand for? _____

2. What does SPF stand for? _____

3. How much sunscreen should you use? _____

4. How often should you use sunscreen? _____

5. What do you think *opaque* means? _____

Big Fish

Write a story about what is happening in this picture. Use the title to guide you.

_____

_____

_____

_____

_____

_____

_____

_____

_____

_____

_____

_____

_____

_____

Itching for Insulin

Diabetes is a disease in which there is too much sugar in the blood. To regulate sugar, your body produces a hormone called insulin. Insulin helps break down the food you eat. Every time you eat something, your body turns that food into glucose, which is a kind of sugar. This glucose is what fuels your body and gives you energy. But for those with diabetes, their bodies either have trouble producing enough insulin or are not able to use the insulin they do produce. Either way, the result is the same: too much sugar is built up.

Having too much sugar in your blood can damage every part of your body. People with diabetes have a much higher risk of heart attack, stroke, blindness, kidney failure, and blood circulation problems.

Type-1 diabetes is also called juvenile diabetes because most people develop it as children. With type-1 diabetes, the immune system attacks the cells that make insulin. Without the insulin, diabetes develops. About 5–10% of diabetes patients have type-1 diabetes.

The remainder of diabetes patients has type-2 diabetes. Unlike type 1, those with type-2 diabetes have bodies that produce insulin. But the body doesn't make enough insulin or just is unable to use what insulin it has.

Unfortunately, there is currently no cure for diabetes. There are medications available to help control the disease. And some patients can even just change their diets and exercise regularly to control their diabetes.

Answer the questions about the reading.

1. What is diabetes? _____

_____

2. What causes diabetes? _____

_____

3. What is one effect of diabetes? _____

4. What is the difference between type-1 and type-2 diabetes? _____

_____

Digestive Trip

Every time you swallow a bite of food, the food travels a certain path through your digestive system. Food starts off in the mouth, where the process of chewing begins to break it down. The food is also broken down by chemicals in your saliva.

Next, you swallow your food, and the food enters the esophagus. The esophagus is a long tube that runs from the mouth to the stomach. It uses a process called peristalsis to force food from the throat into the stomach. Peristalsis is a wave-like muscle movement that moves the food. This enables people to eat or drink even while upside-down!

Then your food ends up in the stomach. Inside the stomach, food gets mixed with gastric acid, which helps break it down even further. After the stomach, food moves through the intestines. First, it enters the duodenum, which is the first part of the small intestine. Then it heads to the jejunum and, finally, the ileum, which is the end piece of the small intestine. Several chemicals in the small intestine, such as bile, help break down the food.

Next, food passes into the large intestine, which is connected to the small intestine. The first part of the large intestine is called the cecum. Then food actually moves upward in the ascending colon. Then food travels sideways! It goes across the abdomen in the transverse colon. Finally food goes down again in the descending colon, and then through the sigmoid colon.

By the end of its journey, any remaining food is now a waste product of your body. It is stored in the rectum until you go to the bathroom, when it leaves the body through the anus.

Number the events in the correct order.

_____ Food enters the esophagus.

_____ Then food actually moves upward in the ascending colon.

_____ The process of chewing begins to break down the food.

_____ Waste product is stored in the rectum until you go to the bathroom, when it leaves the body through the anus.

_____ Then food heads to the jejunum.

_____ Inside the stomach, food mixes with gastric acid.

Germ Patrol

Microbes, also known as germs, are all around us at all times. There are many varieties, and most germs are harmless, but some can give you a cold or even food poisoning. You come in contact with them almost everywhere you go. Germs reside in the kitchen, the cafeteria, the gym, and the restroom. But they also hang out in places that are a bit less obvious, such as on your video game console, computer keyboard, phone, doorknobs, handrails, and your pet.

Germs spread faster than you can imagine. After you touch something that someone else has touched, you likely have his or her germs. Let's say you touch a computer keyboard. You may now have the germs of at least the last person who touched that keyboard. Perhaps next you touch a plate. The person who eats off the plate next has the germs! It is an endless cycle.

But there is one simple way to help stop germs from spreading and making you sick: wash your hands! Washing kills the germs that are living on your hands, which stops you from spreading them to others. Washing also prevents you from spreading them to other parts of your body, such as your eyes.

Wash your hands before doing things like preparing food, eating, or touching a wound. Wash your hands after doing such things as using the restroom, blowing your nose, or playing with a dog. This basic action will help keep you, and those around you, healthy and happy.

Answer the questions about the reading.

1. What is another word for *germ*? _____

2. Where are germs found? _____

3. What is one effect that germs have on people? _____

_____

4. How can you protect yourself from harmful germs? _____

5. Identify a time when you should wash your hands. _____

_____

Germ Ginny

There is nothing that Ginny despises more than germs. "Germs make you sick," Ginny always says, "and I don't care to feel sick!"

Ginny goes to great lengths to rid her life of germs. Ginny carries disinfectant hand gel in her purse, and she keeps a second bottle in her car, just in case. Ginny also keeps disinfecting wipes handy at all times: a few in her bag, a bunch at her desk, and some in her car's glove box. She wipes everything with them!

In addition, Ginny insists on washing her hands twenty times per day! She runs water until it is hot, and then she wets her hands and lathers up. Next, she scrubs until it seems like her skin will be scrubbed right off. Then she rinses her hands and dries them on a paper towel. "Never use a hand towel," Ginny reminds everyone. "Hand towels harbor germs!"

Ginny won't dare hold the handrail on the bus or train, and she refuses to hug and shake hands. "Other people's bodies contain germs!" Ginny chirps. Recently, I saw Ginny use her elbow to hit the button in an elevator, and she explained, "Everyone that gets in here eventually touches that button!" Ginny will not frolic in public places where germs can linger, such as the movie theater or an amusement park. Ginny rarely even dines out.

I understand that Ginny does not care to feel sick—nobody does. But she worries so much about avoiding germs that sometimes I think she is missing out on life!

Write *true* or *false* after each sentence about the story.

1. Ginny won't dare hold the handrail on the bus or train. _____

2. Ginny always dines out. _____

3. Ginny keeps disinfectant hand gel in her car. _____

4. There is nothing that Ginny despises more than germs. _____

5. Ginny must wash her hands twenty times per day! _____

6. Ginny uses her knuckle to hit the button in an elevator. _____

Mount Everest

Mount Everest is the world's highest mountain, making it one of the Seven Wonders of the Natural World. It sits on the border of Nepal and Tibet in Asia, and it is part of the Himalaya mountain range. Mount Everest is famous for its height: it stands at 29,035 feet and rising. That's right—the mountain actually rises a few millimeters each year because of geological forces. Mount Everest is infamous because it is so difficult to climb.

The climate of Mount Everest is severe at best. At its coldest, the summit of Mount Everest is an average temperature of −33° F, but it can drop as low as −76° F. Even in the summer, the average summit temperature is −2° F. The summit never rises above freezing.

Mount Everest also receives much wind and snow. June to September is Indian monsoon season. During these months, wind and precipitation blow in from the Indian Ocean, causing violent snowstorms. In the winter months, the jet stream moves in from the north and hits Mount Everest with hurricane-force winds of more than 177 mph.

Thousands of people have tried to climb Everest, which is a treacherous expedition. The first people to climb Mount Everest successfully were a man from New Zealand named Edmund Hillary and his regional mountain guide, Tenzing Norgay. They did so in 1953. Since that time, more than 700 people have successfully made it to the top. But sadly, at least 150 have died trying.

Answer the questions about the reading.

1. Who were the first people to climb Mount Everest successfully? _____

_____

2. Where is Mount Everest located? _____

3. How high is Mount Everest? _____

4. What mountain range is Mount Everest a part of? _____

5. How cold does it get on Mount Everest? _____

6. Besides temperature, what else makes Mount Everest difficult to climb? _____

_____

Great Barrier Reef

The Great Barrier Reef is one of the Seven Wonders of the Natural World. It is the largest coral reef in the world. The Great Barrier Reef sits off the northeastern coast of Australia and extends for about 1,250 miles. It can even be seen from space!

Corals are simple animals with a soft tubular body, called a polyp. They attach to a surface and have a mouth and ring of tentacles that grab food. Some corals live in large groups called colonies. They create a shared skeleton made of calcium carbonate, also known as limestone.

When a number of corals like this live together, their skeletons combine to form what is known as a coral reef, such as the Great Barrier. The reef stays stationary because sand and even animal shells fill the gaps between the coral skeletons. This creates a solid limestone foundation, and the reef just keeps growing.

The Great Barrier Reef is a truly amazing natural structure. It is the world's largest structure made of living organisms with an area of about 14,300 square miles. The Great Barrier Reef is so large that it makes up about 13 percent of the world's total coral reefs. It is also home to about 1,500 species of fish and other aquatic life.

Unscramble the words mentioned in the reading.

1. sfih _____

2. egrat arbrier rfee _____

3. orcal efre _____

4. esnetlimo _____

5. aatrausli _____

6. skensleto _____

Coloring Coral

Draw a colorful image of what the Great Barrier Reef might look like
through the eyes of a fish or underwater diver.

Grand Canyon

The Grand Canyon is a massive, rocky gorge located in Arizona. The Canyon is about 277 miles long and 18 miles wide. And it is an astounding 6,000 feet deep at its deepest point.

About 6 million years ago, the Colorado River began eroding the rock layers of the Colorado Plateau, thereby carving out the Grand Canyon. The river exposed billions of years' worth of rock, with each layer representing a geological period in the history of the earth. Scientists believe that the oldest rock layers found in the Grand Canyon are more than 2 billion years old, while the top layers are about 250 million years old.

The Grand Canyon is a famous American landmark because of its geological significance and its beauty. The Colorado River did a fine job of creating buttes, mesas, and valleys around the canyon. It is also an extraordinary ecosystem. The Grand Canyon hosts more than 1,500 plant, 355 bird, 89 mammalian, 47 reptile, 9 amphibian, and 17 fish species. Some of these are endemic to the Grand Canyon, which means they can be found only there. The area also contains more than 2,600 documented prehistoric ruins.

A large portion of the Grand Canyon is protected because it is a part of Grand Canyon National Park. The park receives about four million visitors a year, all seeking a glimpse of this natural wonder.

Answer the questions about the reading.

1. Where is the Grand Canyon? _____

2. How deep is the Grand Canyon? _____

3. What formed the Grand Canyon? _____

4. How old are the deepest layers of the Grand Canyon? _____

5. How can you describe something *endemic*? _____

_____

6. About how many people visit the Grand Canyon National Park each year? _____

Victoria Falls

Another of the world's great natural wonders is Victoria Falls, which is located in Africa, on the border of Zambia and Zimbabwe, along the Zambezi River. The waters of the Zambezi pour 19 trillion cubic feet of water per minute into this gorge, which is 1.25 miles wide and 328 feet deep. Victoria Falls is the largest waterfall in the world.

Africans call Victoria Falls *Mosi-oa-Tunya*, which means "smoke that thunders." As they fall, the waters make a loud, thundering spray that looks like a cloud. Victoria Falls  was "discovered" by Europeans in 1855, though of course it had been known to Africans already. A Scottish man named David Livingstone was the first white man to see the falls when he traveled there. He named the waterfall after the Queen of England, Queen Victoria.

Victoria Falls is part of the 5,782-acre Victoria Falls National Park. It has become one of the world's popular tourist attractions. People travel there to whitewater raft along the river, to hike, and to observe the natural splendor of the waterfall. Because of the unique scenery and geological interest, the waterfall has been designated a UNESCO World Heritage Site.

Answer the questions about the reading. Write the letter of the answer on the line.

1. On what continent is Victoria Falls? _____

    a. Antartica

    b. Asia

    c. Africa

2. On what river is Victoria Falls? _____

    a. Nile

    b. Zambezi

    c. Amazon

3. Who was the first European to see Victoria Falls? _____

    a. David Livingstone

    b. Robert Livingston

    c. David Beckham

4. What do Africans call Victoria Falls? _____

    a. Oa-tunya-Mosi

    b. Tunya-oa-Mosi

    c. Mosi-oa-Tunya

5. What makes Victoria Falls so special? _____

    a. It is the largest waterfall in the world.

    b. It contains the most wildlife of any waterfall.

    c. It is the smallest waterfall in the world.

6. After whom was the waterfall named? _____

    a. the Queen of France

    b. the Queen of England

    c. the Queen of Africa

Harbor at Rio de Janeiro

Rio de Janeiro is Brazil's second largest city and the country's former capital. The city serves as the cultural heart of the country. Rio de Janeiro is also a financial, commercial, communications, and transportation center.

Perhaps the most impressive aspect of Rio is its harbor. The Harbor at Rio de Janeiro is one of the world's most beautiful natural harbors. It sets a lovely scene of towering mountains and beautiful beaches. The harbor was formed by the Atlantic Ocean, which eroded the soil and rocks along the coast. It is surrounded by low mountain ranges. Its major natural landmarks are Sugarloaf Mountain, which seems to project right out of the water at a shocking angle, and Corcovado Peak, which overlooks the harbor.

The Harbor at Rio de Janeiro is also the home of a massive statue of Jesus Christ, called Christ the Redeemer. The statue sits at the summit of Corcovado Peak.

The Harbor at Rio de Janeiro is also known as Guanabara Bay, which sits in the Atlantic Ocean. The first Europeans to see the harbor area were the Portuguese, on January 1, 1502. *Rio de Janeiro* translates to "River of January." The Portuguese explorers thought the harbor was actually the mouth of a huge river!

Answer the questions about the reading.

1. In what country is the Harbor at Rio de Janeiro? _____

2. How was the harbor formed? _____

_____

3. What is one landmark in the harbor? _____

4. What is a second landmark in the harbor? _____

5. What is another name for the Harbor at Rio de Janeiro? _____

6. What does *Rio de Janeiro* mean in English? _____

Paricutin

The story of Paricutin Volcano in Mexico is an example of the astounding powers of earth.

In 1943, about 200 miles west of Mexico City, Paricutin Volcano literally exploded out of a cornfield. Paricutin is the first volcano to have known witnesses at its birth.

But the volcano was not quiet after its birth. As Paricutin was erupting, its lava flowed toward nearby villages. The slow-moving lava eventually spread over 10 square miles. Within two years, it buried most of the town of Paricutin and partially buried its neighbor town, San Juan Parangricutiro.

The unsuspecting people in the area found that their land and homes were destroyed by lava flow. They lost crops, livestock, and suffered substantial damage to their property. But amazingly, the ash- and lava-filled eruption caused no fatalities.

Paricutin Volcano finally stopped erupting in 1952. During those nine years, it had grown to 10,400 feet, making it the fastest-growing volcano in history. Paricutin is the most recent volcano to have formed on the Western Hemisphere, and it is considered one of the Seven Wonders of the Natural World.

Answer the questions about the reading.

1. When was Paricutin Volcano born? _____

2. What makes it so unique? _____

_____

3. In what country is Paricutin? _____

4. What is one way that Paricutin's birth affected people? _____

_____

5. When did Paricutin stop erupting? _____

6. How many people were killed as a result? _____

Cornfield Volcano

Draw an image of Paricutin Volcano erupting out of the middle of a cornfield in Mexico.

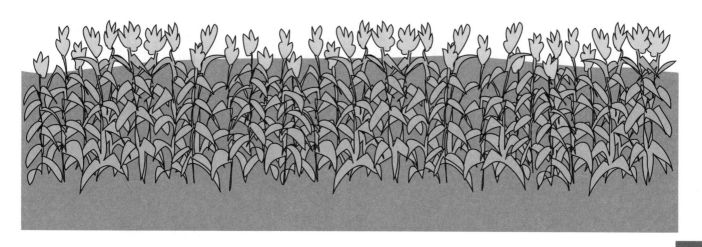

Northern Lights

The Northern Lights, which are also called aurora borealis, are an extraordinary natural phenomenon. They are essentially a light show created by the sun and earth!

The Northern Lights resemble colorful, dancing bands of light in the sky. They occur when particles from the sun collide with gases in earth's atmosphere. The collision energy between the solar particles and the atmospheric gas is emitted as light. The result of many of these collisions is an aurora, or lights that seem to dance across the sky.

The Northern Lights usually occur in northern areas, such as Alaska, but they have been seen as far south as Arizona. A display of aurora borealis can be huge: up to 2,000 miles wide. They can be different shapes and different colors. However, oftentimes the lights are green, red, or purple. This spectacular light show is named after Aurora, who was the Roman goddess of dawn, and Boreas, who was the Greek god of the north wind.

Extensive auroras are doubtlessly beautiful to witness, but they can also cause problems. A significant display sometimes interferes with radio, telephone, and telegraph transmissions!

This natural phenomenon is one of the Seven Wonders of the Natural World, and it also occurs in other parts of the world. When seen in southern areas, these auroras are called Southern Lights.

Find six words from the reading in the word puzzle below.

R	V	A	Q	E	I	O	S	O	U	D	O	Q	O
A	U	R	O	R	A	B	O	R	E	A	L	I	S
R	S	Z	O	I	E	N	L	B	E	Z	M	I	I
G	U	V	D	V	D	V	A	C	V	U	O	Q	D
R	A	N	Q	E	O	C	R	I	U	B	N	R	E
E	C	C	A	O	G	E	T	S	F	E	W	E	O
E	E	F	O	U	W	A	U	E	L	D	E	V	I
N	O	R	T	H	E	R	N	L	I	G	H	T	S
D	Y	Q	B	W	O	T	J	Q	M	I	L	K	K
D	C	G	Z	A	D	H	O	U	T	Z	T	A	Y

Pack Your Bags

We are going on a trip around the globe to see the Seven Wonders of the Natural World! Packing is a big challenge, though, considering the various climates and countries involved.

We'll start in Arizona for a hike through the Grand Canyon. We'll each need to pack three pairs of shorts, one pair of hiking boots, four pairs of socks, four T-shirts, and a backpack.

Then we'll head to Alaska for a peek at the Northern Lights. The temperature is chilly there for much of the year, so we'll each need two pairs of long underwear, one pair of snow boots, a parka, insulated gloves, a hat, a scarf, and three wool sweaters. We'll also need to add water-resistant pants and three pairs of warm socks. To stay warm during our Mount Everest hike in the Himalayas, we'll need a lot of the same gear, so we don't need anything extra for that leg of the trip. Next, to get close to Victoria Falls in Africa, we will each also need a rain poncho and rubber boots.

We'll head back to North America and trek out to a Mexican volcano. We'll need walking shoes, three lightweight T-shirts and two pairs of shorts. Then we'll head south to Rio de Janeiro to see the famed harbor. I'll need some festive gear, such as two flowing dresses, high-heeled shoes, and flowers for my hair. But, we'll also need some of the hiking clothes we packed for Arizona if we're going to Corcovado Peak.

Finally, we'll go to the "land down under" for an underwater view of the Great Barrier Reef. That means we'll each need two swimsuits, flippers, goggles, and our underwater cameras. Okay, I think we're set. See you on the road less traveled!

Answer the questions about the reading.

1. How many pairs of socks are going in the author's suitcase? _____

2. For which site do we need flippers? _____

3. How many pairs of boots are going in the author's suitcase? _____

4. For which wonder do we need a rain poncho? _____

5. How many T-shirts are going in the author's suitcase? _____

6. For which site does the author need a dress? _____

Great Pyramid at Giza

The pyramids are some of the most impressive monuments of the ancient world. How an ancient people could build such massive structures is a constant source of fascination. While they are astonishing architectural achievements, the pyramids had a practical purpose. The large pyramids were built as tombs for pharaohs, or rulers, of Egypt.

The largest of the pyramids is called the Great Pyramid at Giza. Egyptologists, or scientists who study Ancient Egypt, believe that the Great Pyramid was built as a tomb for the 4th century BCE pharoah Khufu. The Great Pyramid at Giza stands 481.4 feet tall—almost 50 stories high—and its base covers 13 acres.

The Great Pyramid was constructed from approximately 2 million blocks of stone and took about 20 years to complete. Building it required the labor of between 20,000 and 35,000 workers. Many people once thought that these workers were slaves, but now many archaeologists and engineers think otherwise. They feel that the pyramid-builders were actually paid laborers, many of whom probably took pride in the fact that they were building tombs for pharaohs and queens.

The pharaohs probably employed many skilled laborers, such as architects, masons, metalworkers, and carpenters. They would have also needed many unskilled workers, such as water carriers. Acquiring and transporting the stone used to build the Great Pyramid was quite a difficult task, too. The white limestone was quarried on the other side of the Nile River. The limestone then had to be cut and transported to the building site. The pieces of stone were sent up the Nile on a barge to Giza, and then dragged up ramps to the construction site.

Khufu's Great Pyramid was built after some of the other pyramids at Giza, so its architects used techniques developed by previous builders. Historians have always been astounded at how carefully the Great Pyramid at Giza was constructed. The builders selected a somewhat flat area of bedrock, rather than sand, to provide a stable foundation for the Great Pyramid.

The builders of the Great Pyramid at Giza needed to be certain that the structure was symmetrical, so all the exterior stones' height and width had to be equal. To ensure this, workers trimmed the surfaces carefully so that the blocks fit together. The Great Pyramid is a nearly perfect square at its base. Each of its four corners is aligned with the four points on a compass.

To move the massive blocks of stone upward as the pyramid got taller and taller, workers built large ramps that probably wrapped around the pyramid. The ramps were likely made of a mixture of clay, water, and limestone debris. The blocks were dragged up the ramps and put into place.

When the very last stone was laid on the pyramid's peak, the workers would have dismantled the ramps from the top down, polishing the blocks as they worked their way down to the base. Finally, the Great Pyramid was revealed in its entirety, and it remains one of the Seven Wonders of the Ancient World.

Use the words from the word bank to fill in the blanks.

Nile River	Khufu	compass	skilled laborers
ramps	acres	clay	bedrock

1. Egyptologists believe that the Great Pyramid was built as a tomb for the fourth-century pharoah _____.

2. The pharaohs probably employed many _____, such as architects, masons, metalworkers, and carpenters.

3. Each of the Great Pyramid's four corners is aligned with the four points on a

_____.

4. When the very last stone was laid on the pyramid's peak, the workers would have dismantled the _____ from the top down.

5. The Great Pyramid's builders selected a somewhat flat area of _____, rather than sand, to provide a stable foundation.

6. The ramps were likely made of a mixture of _____, water, and limestone debris.

7. The Great Pyramid's base covers 13 _____.

8. The white limestone was quarried on the other side of the _____.

Inside the Great Pyramid

The interior of the Great Pyramid at Giza is complex. It is a series of passages that lead to several rooms.

Entrance: The entrance to the Great Pyramid at Giza sits 55 feet above the ground. Its height provided difficulty for potential tomb robbers.

King's Chamber: This is the most important room inside the Great Pyramid, as it was the room containing Khufu's body. The King's Chamber is a rectangular room made of red granite. At the time of his burial, objects that the pharoah would have needed in his afterlife would have been left in the chamber. But since then the objects have been removed, and all that remains is the granite sarcophagus in which Khufu was buried. About three feet above the floor, on two walls of the King's Chamber, are shafts that run upward to the exterior of the pyramid. The exact purpose of these shafts is not known, but they may have been air shafts.

Queen's Chamber: Early explorers gave the room this name because they thought it was where the queen was laid to rest. However, that case is unlikely. The Queen's Chamber probably held a statue of the king that represented his spirit. Shafts similar to those in the King's Chamber lead out of the Queen's Chamber. However, these shafts do not extend all the way to the outside of the pyramid. They are blocked off after 213 feet.

Descending Passage: This passage runs from the entrance of the Great Pyramid down into bedrock beneath. About 60 feet from the pyramid entrance, before entering the bedrock, the Descending Passage intersects another corridor, called the Ascending Passage.

Ascending Passage: This passage runs upward for about 129 feet, at which point it levels out and enters the Queen's Chamber.

Grand Gallery: The Grand Gallery probably held some of the large stones that were used to plug passages after the king's funeral.

Match each term to its description.

Ascending Passage   held some of the large stones that were used to plug passages after the king's funeral

Grand Gallery   runs from the entrance of the Great Pyramid down into bedrock beneath

Queen's Chamber   on two walls of the King's Chamber, run upward to the exterior of the pyramid

Descending Passage   probably held a statue of the king that represented his spirit

King's Chamber   runs upward for about 129 feet

air shafts   the room in which Khufu's body was placed

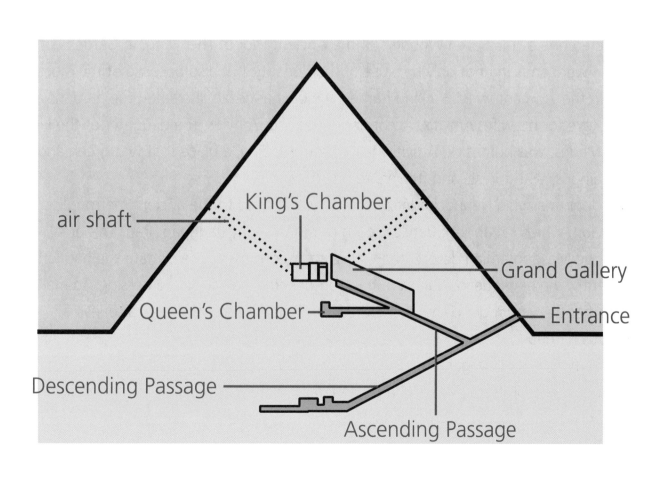

Hanging Gardens of Babylon

The Hanging Gardens of Babylon were built in the 7th century BCE and are considered one of the Seven Wonders of the Ancient World. The Hanging Gardens of Babylon were amazing not only because of their beauty, but also because of their location.

In the 7th century BCE a king named Nebudchadnezzar II created the gardens as a sign of love for his wife, Amyitis. According to legend, Amyitis, the daughter of the king of the Medes, was homesick. Amyitis hailed from Medina, a place that was green and mountainous, with forests and flowers to be enjoyed.

Upon marrying Nebudchadnezzar II, Amyitis moved to the ancient metropolis of Babylon, which sat about 50 miles south of modern-day Baghdad, Iraq. This area was in the Mesopotamian desert, and was in stark contrast to the climate she had left. Apparently, the new queen found the flat, sun-baked desert to be depressing. To make Amyitis happier and more comfortable the king decided to building her a series of gorgeous gardens.

Many think of the gardens as an otherworldly creation that hung in the air somehow. But experts agree that the gardens were actually built on a mountainside, and draped down, rather than actually "hanging."

The Hanging Gardens of Babylon have become legendary. Stories of them spread throughout the ancient world, and ancient writers recorded numerous descriptions of the gardens, but some doubt whether this paradise of the past ever existed. There are no historical records of it, other than stories. Excavations at Babylon have not found any trace of this desert oasis. In addition, another story circulating among scholars is that the gardens were built not by Nebudchadnezzar II, but rather by the Assyrian queen Semiramis. This is why the gardens have sometimes been referred to as the "Gardens of Semiramis."

Regardless, even the notion of the Hanging Gardens of Babylon is amazing. They were essentially impossible to create because of the climate, but they remain in the minds of many as a botanical beauty created in the middle of an uninviting desert landscape.

Answer the questions about the reading.

1. Who ordered the Hanging Gardens of Babylon to be built? _____

_____

2. Why were the Hanging Gardens of Babylon created? _____

_____

3. Did the Hanging Gardens of Babylon actually hang? Explain. _____

_____

4. Where in the world were the gardens? _____

_____

5. Why was their location significant? _____

_____

6. Name one reason why some think that the gardens never existed. _____

_____

Temple of Artemis at Ephesus

The Temple of Artemis at Ephesus was one of the most stunning structures of the ancient world. This wonder of the world was a trophy of Greek civilization.

 The temple was created to honor Artemis, the Greek goddess of hunting and fertility. The construction of the Temple of Artemis began around 550 BCE and was sponsored by Croesus, the Lydian king. The architect Cherisphron designed the temple, which took 120 years to complete. It was located in Ephesus, where the country of Turkey sits today.

The temple was made of marble and featured 106 marble, Ionic-style columns. Each column stood 67 feet tall. In all, the temple was 360 feet high and 180 feet wide. Its front was decorated with bronze statues sculpted by the most skilled artists of the time.

The Temple of Artemis overlooked a courtyard, which served as a marketplace for people to trade their goods. The temple was also a house for worship of Artemis. People came to deliver gifts at the temple and to behold its wonder.

But, the fate of the Temple of Artemis was to be destroyed repeatedly. A man named Herostatus hoped to make his name immortal, so in 356 BCE, he burned the temple to the ground. The temple was reconstructed on the site, but it was destroyed again by the Goths in 262 CE. Finally, in 401 CE, Christians demolished what remained of the Temple of Artemis.

Complete each sentence about the reading. Circle the letter of the answer.

1. The Temple of Artemis was built by the _____ civilization.

   a. Greek

   b. Roman

   c. Turkish

2. Artemis was the god of _____.

   a. trees and plants

   b. the sun and moon

   c. hunting and fertility

3. A man named Herostatus hoped to make his name immortal, so in 356 BCE, he _____ the temple.

   a. burned

   b. blew up

   c. tore down

4. The Temple of Artemis at Ephesus was located in present-day _____.

   a. Greece

   b. Turkey

   c. Iraq

Statue of Zeus at Olympia

Perhaps the most inspiring of all of the Seven Wonders of the Ancient World is the Statue of Zeus at Olympia. People have said of the statue, "Whereas we greatly admire the other six wonders, we kneel in front of this one in reverence."

Zeus was a Greek god—the most powerful of the Olympian gods, in fact. To show their respect for him, the Council of Olympia commissioned the statue.

The Statue of Zeus nearly filled the Temple at Olympia, which is the building that sheltered the statue. The head of the seated Zeus almost touched the ceiling inside the temple, and once someone said that if Zeus were to come to life and stand upright, he'd push the roof off! The temple was built around 430 BCE by the architect Libon and it is located on what is now the west coast of Greece.

Phidias, a renowned Greek sculptor, carved this monument to the Greek god. At about 43 feet tall, the Statue of Zeus at Olympia was carved from ivory and then plated with gold. Zeus sat on a throne made of cedar wood, which was also inlaid with ivory, gold, ebony, and precious jewels. Zeus's right hand held a statue of Nike, the goddess of victory. Zeus's left hand held a shining scepter, or staff, on which an eagle was perched.

Scholars believe that the statue remained in the temple for more than 800 years. It was eventually destroyed, but the circumstances are not clear. Some scholars believe that the statue was destroyed in a fire in the temple in either 170 BCE or the 5th century CE. But some argue that the statue was carried off to Constantinople, where it was later destroyed in the great fire of the Lauseion around the year 462. Nonetheless, only a few columns uncovered during nineteenth- and twentieth-century archaeological digs remain of this famous tribute to Zeus.

Answer the questions about the reading.

1. In what modern country was the Statue of Zeus at Olympia built? _____

2. How long did the statue remain there? _____

3. Who designed the temple that housed the statue? _____

4. Who carved the statue? _____

5. How tall was the Statue of Zeus at Olympia? _____

6. What did Zeus hold in his right hand? _____

Colossus of Rhodes

The Colossus of Rhodes was an enormous bronze statue commissioned by the people of Rhodes, one of the Greek islands. *Colossus* means "a statue of gigantic size and proportions." With it, the citizens of Rhodes sought to honor their sun god, Helios. They believed that Helios had helped ward off attacking nations.

In about 294 BCE, the sculptor Chares of Lindos began building the Colossus. Chares began by making a small model of the statue, and then he worked his way up to larger versions. After 12 years of work, the Colossus of Rhodes was finally completed, and it was a splendor to behold. The Colossus stood 110 feet high on a 50-foot marble block that overlooked the harbor. Its interior contained stone columns that helped keep the statue upright. Some archaeologists also think that the builders used ramps, in much the same way that the Ancient Egyptian pyramids were built.

The Colossus of Rhodes stood proudly at the entrance to Rhodes harbor for about 56 years. In about 226 BCE, however, an earthquake struck Rhodes and the Colossus broke into pieces. But visitors to Rhodes were still awed by the statue as it lay in ruins on the ground for another 900 years.

In the 7th century, Arabs conquered Rhodes, and this marked the end of the Colossus. The fallen remains of the Colossus may have been sold. Stories say that 900 camels were required to cart away all the stone, iron, and bronze that once made up the Colossus of Rhodes, a symbol of the city's former glory.

Write *true* or *false* after each statement from the reading.

1. The Colossus of Rhodes stood proudly at the entrance to Rhodes harbor for about 65 years. _____

2. *Colossus* means "a statue of small size and proportions." _____

3. The citizens of Rhodes sought to honor their sun god, Helios. _____

4. The Colossus stood 110 feet high on a 50-foot marble block. _____

5. The Colossus was located in Rome. _____

6. Some archaeologists think that the builders used ramps, in much the same way that the Ancient Egyptian pyramids were built. _____

Pharos of Alexandria

The Pharos of Alexandria was a lighthouse located on the ancient island of Pharos. This island was just off the coast of the Egyptian city of Alexandria. While the lighthouse was a beautiful architectural structure, it was also one of the only Seven Wonders of the Ancient World that served a practical purpose: guiding sailors. The Pharos lit the way for sailors navigating the harbor into Alexandria.

The Pharos of Alexandria was the idea of Greek ruler Ptolemy Soter. It was designed by architect Sostratus of Cnidus, and construction of the lighthouse began around 300 BCE. The lighthouse was built with blocks of light-colored stone and it had three parts, one built right on top of another. The total height was about 400 feet, making the Pharos of Alexandria the tallest manmade structure on earth for many centuries.

Inside the base of the lighthouse was a cylinder that carried fuel to the top. A fire burning from the top of the structure guided ships during the night. During the day, polished bronze mirrors reflected sunlight out to sea for the same reason.

Unfortunately, several earthquakes destroyed most of the famed lighthouse in the 14th century. In 1480, the Sultan of Egypt tore down the remaining structure and used its stone and marble to build a fort on the same site.

Answer the questions about the reading.

1. What was the practical purpose of the Pharos of Alexandria? _____

_____

2. How did it serve this purpose? _____

_____

3. Where was it located? _____

4. What happened in the 14th century? _____

5. When was the Pharos of Alexandria built? _____

6. What was significant about its height? _____

_____

Mausoleum at Halicarnassus

Another of the Seven Wonders of the Ancient World was the Mausoleum at Halicarnassus. The building served as a tomb for the Persian King Mausolos of Caria. Today the word *mausoleum* describes any grand tomb, but it originally meant "in honor of Mausol."

This magnificent tomb sat in the city of Halicarnassus in Asia Minor. It was located near the modern city of Bodrum in Turkey. The Mausoleum was exceptional both for its beauty and its massive size.

When King Mausolos died in 353 BCE, his grieving wife, Artemisia, decided to honor her husband by building a tomb larger than any that had ever been built. The task took many years, but the result was noteworthy.

The Mausoleum at Halicarnassus was designed by the Greek architects Satyrus and Pythius. The tomb was about 150 feet high and surrounded by 36 Ionic columns. It was built of white alabaster, adorned with gold, and was guarded by stone lions at its stairway. On its roof was a large stone sculpture of Mausolus and Artemisia standing in a chariot.

For about 16 centuries, the Mausoleum at Halicarnassus remained fairly intact. However, during the Middle Ages, much of the Mausoleum was damaged by earthquake. Then, in the 15th century, religious crusaders destroyed what remained of the Mausoleum because it represented a religion and era of which they did not approve.

Unscramble the words mentioned in the reading.

1. misiartea _____

2. eegrk _____

3. mtob _____

4. maoleumus _____

5. hrnaalicassus _____

6. uetrky _____

Just Wondering

Each of the Seven Wonders of the Ancient World was built for a grand reason, and most honored a god or ruler. If you were to pick a person to build a monument for, who would it be and why? What would your monument look like, and where would it be located? Write about it on the lines below.

_____

_____

_____

_____

_____

_____

_____

_____

_____

_____

The Newest Wonders of the World

As you read the passage, fill in each blank with any word from the correct part of speech. Have fun!

Recently, _____ New Wonders of the _____ were
          NUMBER   NOUN

chosen. The contest was organized by the _____ Foundation—the
                                            SILLY WORD

_____ child of _____ filmmaker and museum
PART OF THE BODY   LANGUAGE

_____ _____. He felt it was _____ to
OCCUPATION   CELEBRITY (MALE)   ADJECTIVE

protect _____ heritage across the _____.
       PLURAL NOUN   NOUN

To choose the _____, people all over the world
              PLURAL NOUN

_____. They did so by _____ online and by
VERB (PAST TENSE)   VERB ENDING IN "ING"

_____.
VERB ENDING IN "ING"

Not all _____ agree with the decision, but the poll attracted almost
       PLURAL NOUN

_____ votes. And the _____ doesn't lie!
NUMBER   NOUN

El Castillo

On the Yucatan Peninsula in Mexico lies Chichén Itzá. Looming in the center of the ancient city is El Castillo, which means "the castle" in Spanish. Also called the Pyramid of Kukulkán, it is a 79-foot stone pyramid erected by the Mayan people around 1000 CE. The pyramid has an amazing purpose: it tells time.

Twice a year, thousands of tourists gather at El Castillo to witness the astronomical phenomenon it has become famous for. They watch in awe as light and shadow create the appearance of a snake slithering down the stairway of the pyramid. The "shadow snake" is composed of triangular shadows cast by the stepped terraces of the pyramid. Carved at the base of the stairway are large snakehead sculptures. As the sun moves and the shadows slither down the stairway, the body of the shadow snake unites with one of the carved heads.

The existence of this shadow snake and the positioning and architecture of the pyramid suggest that its Mayan builders had an understanding of astronomy. The snake is created because the west side of the pyramid faces the zenith passage, or the path the sun takes from sunset to sunrise through the zenith, which is an imaginary point directly overhead. This event happens twice a year in Mexico, on the spring and autumn equinoxes.

Each of El Castillo's four stairways has 91 steps, with a final step at the top. This makes for a total of 365, which is the number of days in a solar year. Ninety-one days also separate each of the four phases of the annual solar cycle: the winter solstice, the spring equinox, the summer solstice, and the autumn equinox. The Mayan people likely used El Castillo to track the seasons and solar events, which would have let them know when to plant, harvest, and perform ceremonies.

Answer the questions about the reading.

1. What culture built El Castillo? _____

2. What happens twice a year in Mexico? _____

3. What is the effect at El Castillo? _____

_____

4. What did El Castillo allow people to do? _____

_____

Christ the Redeemer

In the Harbor of Rio de Janeiro, Brazil, stands a massive statue of Jesus which overlooks the city from 2,340 feet up. The statue, called Christ the Redeemer, is not only one of Rio's most famous sites, but one of the world's as well.

The French sculptor Paul Landowski was commissioned to create Christ the Redeemer. It stands 100 feet high and rests on a pedestal 20 feet high. The granite sculpture of Christ has his arms outstretched, as if embracing the city.

Christ the Redeemer was inaugurated on October 12, 1931. It has become a symbol of the city of Rio de Janeiro. It represents not only the religious beliefs of the people of Brazil, but also their warmth. Just as Christ the Redeemer does, the Brazilians receive visitors with open arms. Christ the Redeemer is located on the top of Corcovado Mountain. Today, it can be reached by either road or railway.

In 2006, the Roman Catholic Church named Christ the Redeemer a religious pilgrimage site and declared it a Catholic sanctuary.

Match each number to its description.

100   year when Christ the Redeemer was declared a Catholic sanctuary

1931   distance above Rio de Janeiro that Christ the Redeemer stands

2006   height of Christ the Redeemer's pedestal

20   height of the statue portion of Christ the Redeemer

2,340   year when Christ the Redeemer opened

Roman Colosseum

The Colosseum in Rome was the largest and most famous Ancient Roman amphitheater, or open auditorium. On this site fought the famed Roman gladiators. The Roman Colosseum was built around 80 CE and its general design is still used for many modern sports stadiums.

The Roman Colosseum was an ellipse, or uneven circular shape. Its elliptical shape prevented the players from retreating to a corner, while also allowing the spectators to be close to the action. The Colosseum measured 617 feet long, 512 feet wide, and 157 feet high. It was constructed of stone and had eighty arches built on each of the structure's first three levels.

Seating was divided into rising sections. The first level was for the Roman senators and the emperor. The second level was for other Roman aristocrats. The third level was divided into sections: a lower part for wealthy citizens and an upper part for poor ones. The very top of the Roman Colosseum was standing room for lower-class women.

The Roman Colosseum had one particularly inventive feature: a cooling system. It consisted of a rope net covered in canvas. This cloth flap covered two-thirds of the arena and sloped down toward the center to catch the wind and provide a breeze for the audience. Sailors on special platforms pulled the ropes to move the flap.

The Roman Colosseum stayed intact until about 217 CE, when it was damaged by fire. Then it was the victim of several earthquakes between 442 and 1349 that continued to destroy the structure. Today, the public can view its ruins.

Answer the questions about the reading.

1. What shape was the Roman Colosseum and why was it useful? _____

_____

2. What was an inventive feature of the Roman Colosseum? _____

3. Who sat on the second level of the Roman Colosseum? _____

4. Who fought in the Roman Colosseum? _____

5. What destroyed the Roman Colosseum? _____

_____

Taj Mahal

The Taj Mahal is a mausoleum, or grand tomb, located in Agra, India, on the southern bank of the Yamuna River. The Taj Mahal is considered one of the most beautiful buildings in the world. It was built by the Mughal emperor Shah Jahan in memory of his wife, Arjumand Banu Bagam, known as Mumtaz Mahal.

Arjumand Banu Bagam died in 1629, and the construction of the Taj Mahal commenced shortly thereafter. By about 1643, the mausoleum was complete and the surrounding complex of buildings and formal gardens was complete by about 1653.

 The Taj Mahal was built from white marble and has four identical facades, each with a large central arch. The structure also has a large bulb-shaped dome in the center, with four smaller domes surrounding it. Leading up to the Taj Mahal is a large sandstone gate inscribed with passages from the Qur'an, the Islamic holy book. Behind the gate and walls that surround the main structure are the formal gardens. Canals divide the gardens into four equal parts, each containing flowerbeds, fountains, and cypress trees.

The tomb of Arjumand Banu Bagam stands at the center of an octagonal hall inside the Taj Mahal. The tomb of her husband, who died in 1666, is off to the side. Both tombs are ornately carved and decorated with semiprecious stones.

The Taj Mahal still stands today, and is highly regarded as an astounding structure.

Write *fact* or *opinion* after each statement about the reading.

1. The tomb of Arjumand Banu Bagam stands at the center of an octagonal hall inside the Taj Mahal. _____

2. The Taj Mahal is the most beautiful building in the world. _____

3. The Taj Mahal is a mausoleum located in Agra, India. _____

4. The Taj Mahal is an astounding structure. _____

5. Leading up to the Taj Mahal is a large sandstone gate with inscriptions from the Qur'an on it. _____

6. The Taj Mahal was built from white marble and has four identical facades, each with a large central arch. _____

Wondrous Wall

The Great Wall of China is the largest manmade monument in existence. It is so large that it can even be seen from space! It stretches across the mountains of northern China, winding north of Beijing. The Chinese term for the wall is *Wan-Li Qang-Qeng*, which means "10,000-Li-Long Wall." 10,000 Li equals about 3,106 miles.

The Great Wall of China is made from various types of rocks and packed earth. The process of building it was so tremendous and time consuming that it was impossible to build it with uniform tools and materials. So, the wall reflects local resources and skill levels. Its thickness ranges from 15 to 30 feet and it is up to 25 feet tall in certain places.

The Great Wall of China was built more than 2,000 years ago as a form of protection from possible enemies. The first emperor of China, Qin Shi Huangdi, wanted to create a united defense system and keep the Mongol tribes out of China. He ordered that four old fortification walls along the north of China be connected and extended. Armies could then be stationed along the wall as a first line of defense against invasion. They could fire off shots as an early signal that would warn others about an attack.

During the Ming Dynasty, from 1368 to 1644, the Great Wall was enlarged further. After that, the wall slowly became less useful as a form of defense. With new war strategies and more powerful weapons, the Wall was no longer an effective way to protect people. The Great Wall of China still stands today, telling the story of a glorious history.

Answer the questions about the reading.

1. How long is the Great Wall of China? _____

2. Why was it built? _____

3. Why is it made of different materials? _____

_____

4. Who began the construction of the Great Wall of China? _____

5. What dynasty finished the Great Wall of China's construction? _____

Petra's Power

The ancient Arabian city of Petra served as the capital of the Nabataean empire of King Aretas IV. Petra was the stronghold and treasure city of the Nabataean people. It was located in what is now southwestern Jordan.

Petra means "city of rock" in Greek. It was indeed an invincible fortress, but it was also a great natural beauty with magnificent monuments. Leading up to this wondrous city was a ravine with towering rocky walls. Carved out of these rock walls are ancient structures. One of these structures is a semicircular theater, modeled after Greek-Roman ones, that seated about 3,000 to 4,000 spectators.

Rows of tombs are carved out of the solid stone of the city. And what is perhaps the most famous monument in Petra was the Khaznet Firaoun temple, also known as the Treasury of the Pharaohs.

Petra was the capital of the Nabataean kingdom from the 4th century BCE until the 2nd century CE. Then the Romans conquered Petra in 106 CE. The city continued to flourish in the 2nd and 3rd centuries, but in the 7th century, the Muslims conquered Petra. The city was later captured by the Crusaders and gradually fell into ruin. But what does remain of this grand ancient city is proof of its former power, wealth, and people.

Complete each sentence about the reading. Circle the letter of the answer.

1. Petra was the capital city of the _____.

    a. Mongol empire

    b. Jordanian empire

    c. Nabataean empire

2. *Petra* is Greek for _____.

    a. "city of rock"

    b. "city of angels"

    c. "city by the sea"

3. In the 7th century, the _____ conquered Petra.

    a. Crusaders

    b. Muslims

    c. Jews

4. Petra included a semicircular theater, modeled after _____.

    a. Greek-Roman ones

    b. Egyptian ones

    c. Muslim ones

Machu Picchu

Machu Picchu was an ancient Incan city situated in the Andes Mountains, deep in the Amazon jungle about 50 miles northwest of what is now Cusco, Peru. Machu Picchu is sometimes referred to as "the city in the clouds" because it stands on a ridge between two peaks about 1,950 feet above the Urubamba River below.

Machu Picchu is considered one of the most amazing creations of the Inca Empire. Covering about five square miles, it was built around a central plaza and linked by several stairways. Most of the structures at Machu Picchu have one room and are made of stone. They are arranged around courtyards and demonstrate exceptional craftsmanship. Some of the larger structures at Machu Picchu were probably used for religious purposes.

While Machu Picchu is now a world-renowned tourist site, that was not always the case. Machu Picchu was a "lost city" for more than three centuries. It was rediscovered in 1911 by American explorer Hiram Bingham.

Some historians believe that Machu Picchu was built in the 15th century by the Incan Emperor Pachacútec. The Incas may have abandoned it because of an outbreak of smallpox. This Incan wonder also might have been the last refuge of Incas fleeing the Spanish invaders. However, Machu Picchu is not mentioned in the writings of the Spanish conquerors of Peru, so the time of its occupancy remains unclear.

Answer the questions about the reading.

1. What culture built Machu Picchu? _____

2. In what modern country is the ancient city located? _____

3. Why is Machu Picchu sometimes called "the city in the clouds"? _____

_____

4. When was Machu Picchu rediscovered? _____

5. When do some historians think the city was built? _____

6. Why was the city possibly abandoned? _____

79

The Cheddars

The Cheddars are a family of mice that lives in the basement of my high-rise apartment building. They prefer to keep to themselves, showing their faces only when they are in search of a meal or if there is a flood down there. While most people detest mice and consider them mere rodents, I have befriended the Cheddars.

I often find that I have to turn a deaf ear when the tenants in the building speak badly of the Cheddars. "There were foul rodents near the washing machine this morning!" they'll proclaim, or, "I swatted at a renegade mouse with my broom yesterday. It was contaminating the place!" They assume that every mouse is dirty or smelly. But I know for certain that the Cheddars bathe daily. They take a dip in the washing machines and then dry off under the vent to make their coats fluffy.

I think if more people in the building knew how much the Cheddars do for them, they would be a bit nicer to my furry little friends. You see, the Cheddars are the building's tiny maintenance crew. Whenever something breaks, the Cheddars are on the scene to resolve the problem as quickly as their little paws are able.

Just last week, the hot water heater was out of service during the morning, when all the adults in the apartment building were trying to bathe and dress for work. Mr. Cheddar, known as Mac to his friends, woke his sleeping family as soon as he heard the shouts of disgruntled tenants being doused with cold water. The four of them crept into the inner workings of the water boiler and tinkered around until they found the broken part. At which point, Mr. Cheddar scampered over to his stash of spare parts to fetch a replacement.

And when we received a late-winter snowfall last March, who do you think was out in the cold with children's sand shovels, clearing the front steps and sidewalk before the storm even ended? That's right! Mac, his wife Martha, and the two Cheddar children, Minnie and Mickey.

Let this be a lesson to all those who underestimate a mouse. The one you're trying to lure into a trap might just be the same creature fixing your water boiler!

Answer the questions about the story.

1. What does the word *befriended* in paragraph 1 mean? _____

_____

2. What does the word *disgruntled* in paragraph 4 mean? _____

_____

3. What does the word *underestimate* in paragraph 6 mean? _____

_____

4. What does the word *detest* in paragraph 1 mean? _____

_____

5. What does the word *contaminating* in paragraph 2 mean? _____

_____

6. What does the word *doused* in paragraph 4 mean? _____

_____

7. What does the word *renegade* in paragraph 2 mean? _____

_____

8. What does the word *resolve* in paragraph 3 mean? _____

_____

81

Mac's Mac and Cheese Recipe

Ingredients:

3 tablespoons butter

$2\frac{1}{2}$ cups no-bake macaroni

1 teaspoon salt

$\frac{1}{4}$ teaspoon pepper

1 quart milk

$\frac{1}{2}$ pound shredded cheddar cheese

Directions:

1. Melt butter in a baking dish.
2. Pour macaroni into melted butter.
3. Stir until butter coats macaroni.
4. Add salt, pepper, cheese, and milk to macaroni.
5. Bake, uncovered, at 325 degrees for $1\frac{1}{2}$ hours until golden brown and creamy.

Number the recipe steps in the correct order.

_____ Stir until butter coats macaroni.

_____ Bake, uncovered, at 325 degrees for $1\frac{1}{2}$ hours until golden brown and creamy.

_____ Melt butter in a baking dish.

_____ Add salt, pepper, cheese, and milk to macaroni.

_____ Pour macaroni into melted butter.

Choose one ingredient from the recipe and predict what might happen if you forgot to use it.

_____

_____

Mighty Mice

The mouse is a small rodent that can be found in almost any environment, all over the world. But mice usually live either in fields or in human habitats. Mice are territorial mammals that are social with each other but timid with other animals and humans. Mice eat and can damage large quantities of food, and they are also known to spread disease.

Mice will eat almost anything, which makes them omnivores. They eat anything from seeds and grass to fruit and bugs. They also have many natural predators, including cats, dogs, owls, hawks, and humans.

Mice can range from 3 to 14 inches long, which includes the length of their tails. They may weigh between $\frac{1}{4}$ and 2 ounces and range in color from white to brown to gray. Most mice have pointed snouts, long whiskers, round ears, and long, thin tails. Their front teeth grow throughout their life and must be worn down, which is why they gnaw on hard things.

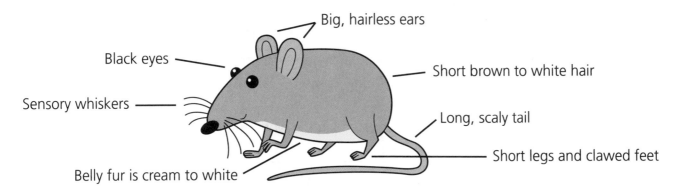

Answer the questions about the reading.

1. Where can mice be found? _____

2. What do mice eat? _____

3. How long are mice? _____

4. Why do mice chew on hard objects? _____

_____

5. Name one natural predator of mice. _____

6. How much do mice weigh? _____

Mouse on Your Desk!

Used with a personal computer, a computer mouse is a device that has a graphical user interface (GUI) to point to things onscreen. Commonly, a computer's user operates a mouse with one hand in order to move a cursor over images or text on a computer screen. A mouse has buttons that activate, open, or move icons when they are displayed under the cursor.

A computer mouse is often attached to the computer through a universal serial bus (USB) port, either through a cord or wirelessly. The USB allows the mouse to report its position at a very high rate. Mice have a multidirectional detection device on the bottom. Moving the mouse along a surface is what enables the user to control an onscreen cursor.

Notebook or laptop computers often have a mouse built into the computer's keyboard. This mouse serves the same function as if it were connected externally.

An external computer mouse has a casing with a flat bottom and is designed to be held with one hand. It usually has one or two buttons on the top, which are "clicked" to create commands or choose items displayed on the computer's screen.

Many computer mice also have a vertical wheel mounted on top, between the two buttons. These wheels allow the user to quickly scroll up and down a screen.

Find six terms from the reading in the word puzzle below.

C	F	O	X	M	O	U	S	E	F
R	V	A	Q	E	I	O	A	O	U
J	S	C	R	E	E	N	W	N	F
R	S	Z	O	I	E	N	I	B	E
B	U	T	T	O	N	S	O	C	V
T	A	N	Q	E	O	C	S	U	U
E	C	C	A	O	G	A	T	R	F
B	E	L	O	U	W	F	U	S	B
R	I	I	H	M	O	N	D	O	S
D	Y	C	B	W	E	V	J	R	M
D	C	K	Z	A	D	Z	O	U	T

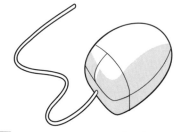

Mouse in the City

There once was a mouse who loved his home in the country. That was until his cousin from the city came to visit him. The city mouse told his country cousin, "In the city, we enjoy the finer things in life. I dine on cheese, fish, and bread. I have as much as I want, whenever I want it."

The country mouse was no longer satisfied with his humble abode. He wondered why he scrounged and scraped for food each day. Then he told his cousin, "I'm going to the fine city with you!"

The very next day, the city mouse and the country mouse arrived in the big city. The city mouse shushed his country cousin, "Quiet! The people are afoot. Let us scamper to the kitchen for some cheese and bread." The country mouse's eyes grew wide. Before him lay an incredible feast of leftover treats. "As I said, I live a fine, easy life, my cousin," the city mouse reminded the country mouse.

But just as the cousins were about to bite into a wheel of cheese, in wandered the cat of the house! "Run!" cried the city mouse. "Now! The cat is afoot!"

The country mouse ran for his life straight out the city house and yelled "Back to the country I go! I prefer humble crumbs in comfort more than finery with fear! To each his own!"

Answer the questions about the story.

1. How does the country mouse feel about his life at the beginning of the story?

_____

2. How does the city mouse make the country mouse feel about himself? _____

_____

3. How does the country mouse feel about the city? _____

_____

4. What would you say the moral, or lesson, of this story is? _____

_____

Mickey Mouse

Mickey Mouse is likely the world's most famous cartoon character. He was created by American animator Walt Disney. In 1928, Mickey Mouse first appeared in a silent short movie called *Steamboat Willy*. He became wildly popular, appearing in cartoons, feature films, comic strips, and books.

But Mickey Mouse isn't just a two-dimensional drawing. This mouse has a big personality! Historically, Mickey Mouse is a "good guy" with a sunny outlook on life and a boyish and enthusiastic nature. Mickey Mouse always shows positive values. He represents the ideal person many people would like to be. Mickey Mouse is also humble, despite his enormous success (and ears!).

Fun Facts about Mickey Mouse

Hobbies	Pet	Girlfriend	Catchphrases
sports sorcery spending time with friends	Pluto, the dog	Minnie Mouse	"Oh, boy!" "Aw-gee" "Sheesh!" "Uh-oh!"

Answer the questions about the reading.

1. When did Mickey Mouse make his first public appearance? _____

2. Who created Mickey Mouse? _____

3. Describe one aspect of his personality. _____

_____

4. Draw a picture of Mickey Mouse and his friends, such as Minnie and Pluto, in the space below. (Hint: Use a quarter and two dimes to draw his head.)

Telephone Manners

It is important to know how to conduct yourself on the telephone. The following are important tips for being safe, polite, and professional.

- ☎ Always greet the caller with "Hello" when you answer the telephone.

- ☎ Do not yell into the telephone. If you must summon another person to pick up, cover the mouthpiece with your hand, or simply hold it away from you.

- ☎ Do not chew gum or eat while speaking on the telephone.

- ☎ Do not hang up on callers. If you must end a call abruptly, excuse yourself and say "good-bye."

- ☎ If you receive an accidental call, or "wrong number," inform the caller that they have reached the wrong person. Then say "good-bye" and hang up.

- ☎ Do not tell callers, especially strangers, that you are home alone.

- ☎ Do not reveal information or answer questions to strangers.

- ☎ If a caller wants to speak to a resident of the household who is unavailable, offer to take a message so that the call may be returned. Write down the caller's name and telephone number, along with any other information they would like to leave.

Write *true* or *false* after each statement about the tips.

1. It is fine to tell someone that no one is home but you. _____

2. When someone reaches the wrong number, you should immediately hang up on him or her. _____

3. If a caller wants to speak to a resident of the household who is unavailable, offer to take a message so that the call may be returned. _____

4. You should always answer a caller's questions, even if you don't know the caller.

_____

5. If you must end a call abruptly, excuse yourself and say "good-bye." _____

6. Do not chew gum or eat while speaking on the telephone. _____

To the Letter

Heading: This section of a letter is at the very top of the paper. It includes your complete mailing address and the date on which you are writing the letter.

Inside address: The inside address is written below the heading. It should include the name of the person the letter will be sent to, that person's title, the name of the business at which they work, and the complete mailing address.

Greeting or Salutation: This section of a letter is where you say hello. It sits below the inside address. There are many ways to greet someone in a business letter, but the most common way is to write *Dear Mr.* if the recipient is male or *Dear Ms.* if the recipient is female. Then insert the person's last name.

Body: The body of a letter is the section in which you write your thoughts or ideas. The body of a business letter should include an introduction, in which you tell the person receiving the letter who you are and why you are writing to him or her. It should also have a middle section. This is where you give your opinion or make a request. State facts and give details that support your thoughts or ideas. Finally, the body of your letter should have a conclusion. Tell the reader what action you would like him or her to take. And always, thank the person or company for reading your letter.

Closing: The closing of a letter is where you say good-bye to the reader. No matter which type of closing you use, always follow it with a comma.

Signature: The signature of a letter is the part in which you write your name.

Read the business letter and then label each section.

_____ 107 Vineyard Lane
                         San Francisco, CA 44704

                         September 14, 2009

Mr. Mark Quigley, Manager
The Sweet Spot
12 January Street   _____
San Francisco, CA 44705

Dear Mr. Quigley: _____

   I often visit your candy and ice cream shop and I'd like to offer a suggestion for how it may be improved.

   I recently visited a famous ice cream parlor in New York City at which there was an ice cream flavor that tastes like cake batter. The taste was exceptional, and the flavor is their bestseller, according to the manager. I think that stocking this type of unique _____ flavor would draw more customers to the Sweet Spot.

   I think that you should consider offering this new flavor of ice cream.

   Thank you very much for your time and consideration.

Sincerely, _____

Avery Scott _____

Avery Scott

How to Write an E-mail

E-mail is a form of written communication that takes place over the Internet. It is an amazing tool and can be very useful. Here are the parts of an e-mail:

To: This is the section of an e-mail where you write the recipient's e-mail address. E-mail addresses start with a series of letters or numbers. Then the symbol @ appears, which stands for "at." Toward the end of an e-mail address there is always a period, or a "dot," and then another series of letters at the end.

Cc: The letters *Cc* stand for "carbon copy." You can insert e-mail addresses into this space, too. This e-mail function allows you to send a message to people in addition to the primary recipient.

Subject: In this section you write the topic of the e-mail message. The subject space should contain only a few words.

Body: This is the section of an e-mail where you write your message. It should have an introduction, a beginning, a middle, an end, and a signature.

Send: Clicking *send* is perhaps the most important part of an e-mail. The send button takes your message to its recipient.

Attachments: Most e-mail programs have an attachment feature. Sometimes a paper clip icon represents this function. This e-mail button allows you to send files along with your e-mail message. You can send things such as documents and pictures.

Read the e-mail and then label each section.

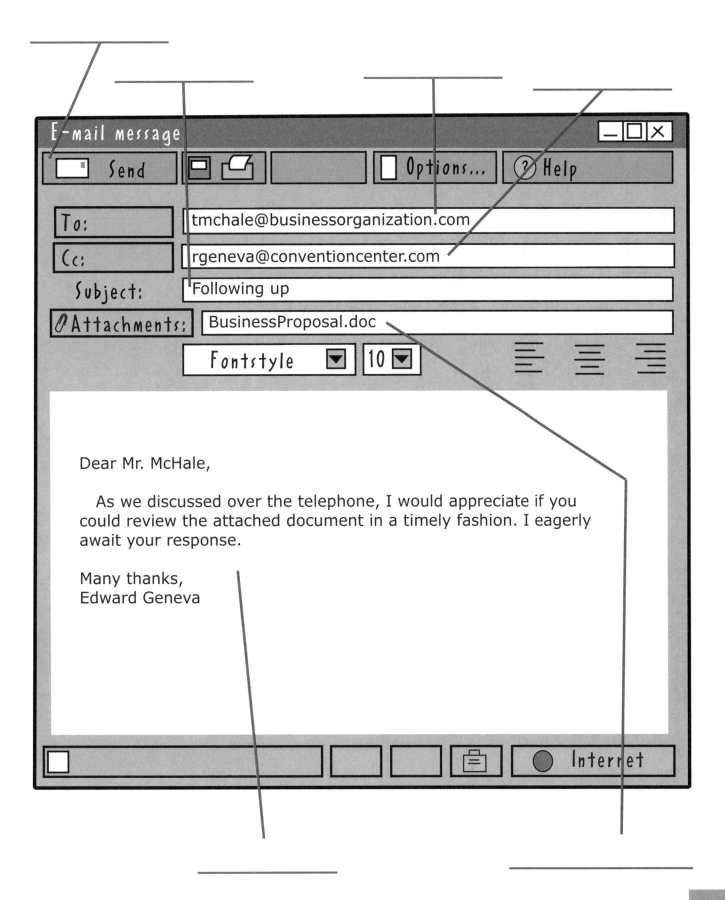

E-mail message

Send Options... (?) Help

To: tmchale@businessorganization.com

Cc: rgeneva@conventioncenter.com

Subject: Following up

Attachments: BusinessProposal.doc

Fontstyle 10

Dear Mr. McHale,

As we discussed over the telephone, I would appreciate if you could review the attached document in a timely fashion. I eagerly await your response.

Many thanks,
Edward Geneva

Internet

E-mail Etiquette

Like any other form of writing, there are certain ways in which e-mail should be written.

Get to the point: Even if you are writing an e-mail just to say hello to a friend, make it shorter than you would a letter.

Use proper spelling, grammar, and punctuation: E-mails with bad grammar or no punctuation are difficult to read and can sometimes give the wrong meaning.

Do not write in all capital letters: Writing an e-mail message with the caps-lock function is like screaming over e-mail. If you want to emphasize a certain word, only capitalize that word, or place an asterisk (*) on either side of it.

Be careful when using abbreviations and emoticons: If you are writing a formal e-mail, such as one for school or to a person of authority, do not use abbreviations or emoticons, which are happy faces and such.

Do not use e-mail to say anything private or offensive: E-mail is sent over the Internet. The Internet is not a safe or private place. This is especially true if you share a computer or use one in a public place. If you have composed it, a message can almost always be seen by anyone who uses that computer.

Answer the questions about the reading.

1. Why should you avoid writing e-mails in capital letters? _____

_____

2. Why should you not reveal private information over e-mail? _____

_____

3. Is it acceptable to use ☺ in a business e-mail? _____

4. Are very long e-mail messages a good idea? _____

5. Why is it important to use proper spelling, grammar, and punctuation in an e-mail message? _____

Impressionable

First impressions leave a lasting feeling with others, and they can often make a significant difference, whether in creating a friendship or closing a business deal. Here are some points for making a good first impression.

Be focused on others: Showing first-time acquaintances that you are interested in them will make them eager to see you again.

Listen up: Similar to the first point, you should always demonstrate good listening skills. No one likes to feel that they are not being paid attention to, especially when speaking. Maintain eye contact with the speaker and make gestures such as nodding to indicate that you are listening closely to what he or she has to say. Follow up with relevant questions about what the speaker has said.

Name drop: Upon meeting new people, use their names frequently when speaking to them. First, it helps you remember his or her name, especially if you are prone to forgetting names. Second, studies show that people respond positively to hearing their own names.

Dress the part: Appearance counts. Making yourself look neat and presentable shows others that you value them enough to have cleaned up before meeting them.

Speak clearly: Those who hear us speak will judge our intelligence, education, and even leadership capabilities. Not only select your words carefully, but also present them clearly and confidently.

Match each point to its description.

Name drop	Speak clearly and confidently.
Speak clearly	Upon meeting someone new, use their name frequently.
Be focused on others	Maintain eye contact and make gestures.
Dress the part	Show acquaintances that you are interested in them.
Listen up	Groom properly and wear appropriate clothing.

Saying Thanks

It shows appreciation and good manners to send a thank-you note after receiving a gift, receiving a kind favor, or being hosted by another. Here are some tips for writing an appropriate thank-you note.

- Use nice stationery or a note card and write neatly.

- Add a personal touch and be specific. For example, tell the recipient how much you enjoyed the book you received or how much fun you had on his or her sailboat.

- If you received money as a gift, do not mention the amount given.

- It seems obvious, but sometimes people forget the most important part: The words "thank you!"

- Re-read the thank-you note. Check for spelling and grammatical mistakes. If you made an error, write a new note. Do not send a thank-you with cross-outs!

- Send the thank-you note promptly, so that the person receiving it knows how much you appreciate the gesture.

Write a short thank-you note to a relative who sent you a birthday gift.

_____

_____

_____

_____

_____

_____

Chocolate Chip Champs

This recipe makes some of the world's tastiest chocolate chip cookies.

Preheat oven to 375 degrees.

Ingredients:

1 stick unsalted butter

1 cup brown sugar

3 tablespoons granulated sugar

1 egg

3 teaspoons vanilla

2 tablespoons milk

$\frac{1}{2}$ teaspoon baking soda

$\frac{1}{2}$ teaspoon baking powder

$\frac{1}{2}$ teaspoon salt

$1\frac{3}{4}$ cups flour

8 ounces chocolate chips

Directions:

Cream butter and sugar together.
Beat in egg, vanilla, and milk.
Combine dry ingredients in a separate bowl. Then combine with butter mixture.
Drop spoonfuls of dough, about two inches apart, onto a greased cookie sheet.
Bake for 8–10 minutes.

Answer the questions about the recipe.

1. What is the very first thing you should do to make these cookies? _____

_____

2. What do you think would happen if you did not take this step? _____

_____

3. Why do you think it is important to use unsalted butter in this recipe? _____

_____

4. What do you think would happen if you baked the cookies for 20 minutes? _____

_____

The Accidental Cookie

A woman named Ruth Wakefield and her husband were the owners of The Toll House Inn in Whitman, Massachusetts. One evening in 1937, Ruth was making butter cookies for

her guests and decided to make them chocolate flavored, so she cut a Nestlé chocolate bar into small pieces and added them to the cookie dough. Ruth figured that the chocolate would melt and mix into the dough while in the oven, creating a chocolate cookie.

But, to Ruth's surprise, the chocolate bits didn't melt down. She served the cookies, anyway, and they were an enormous hit with the guests at the Toll House Inn. Soon, people began to come to the inn just to eat Ruth's delicious cookies.

Eventually, Ruth approached the Nestlé Company with her recipe for "Chocolate Crunch Cookies." Just like the guests at the Toll House Inn, Nestlé thought the idea was genius. They began printing Ruth's recipe on the back of their chocolate bars and they gave Ruth an endless supply of chocolate so that she could keep making her cookies.

Nestlé wanted to encourage others to use the recipe on their package, so they even began packaging their chocolate bars with a small chopper. By 1939, Nestlé was selling Chocolate Morsels, the pre-chopped bits of chocolate we know today.

Answer the questions about the reading. Write the letter of the answer on the line.

1. What genre, or type of writing, is this reading? _____

   a. folktale
   b. fiction
   c. historical nonfiction

2. What is the main idea of this reading? _____

   a. Nestlé thought the idea was genius.
   b. Sometimes the best ideas aren't planned.
   c. Nestlé wanted to encourage others to use the recipe on their package.

3. Why would Nestlé want to encourage others to use Ruth's recipe? _____

   a. So that people would buy more of their chocolate.
   b. So that Ruth's inn would become more popular.
   c. So that Ruth would go out of business.

4. In what year did Ruth accidentally make her Toll House cookies? _____

   a. 1939
   b. 1937
   c. 1973

O-R-E-O

They have been called "America's favorite cookie," and more recently, "milk's favorite cookie." Either way the cookie crumbles, Oreos are an American classic.

In 1912, the National Biscuit Company (Nabisco) had an idea that would make it the cookie king. It created a cookie by spreading a cream filling between two chocolate disks. The Oreo was born!

Originally, the Oreo was available in both lemon meringue and cream flavors. But the cream filling was much more popular, so Nabisco stopped producing the lemon meringue filling in the 1920s. The original Oreo cookies looked very similar to modern Oreo cookies, although the design on the chocolate cookie's surface was changed a bit over time. The shape and overall look remained the same until the 1970s, when Nabisco began selling different versions of its Oreo cookie, such as the Double Stuf Oreo.

The O-R-E-O jingle, or advertisement song, has become known worldwide. But the origin of the name remains unclear. Even Nabisco isn't sure! Gold was the main color on early Oreo packages, so the name *Oreo* might be from the French word for "gold," which is *or*. But other people claim the name stemmed from the original shape of the test cookies, which was like a small mountain. The Greek word for "mountain" is *oreo*. The name *Oreo* might have even come from taking the letters *re* in cream and placing them between the two letter *o*s in the word *chocolate—OREO*! Regardless of how it acquired its famous name, the Oreo cookie is considered the bestselling cookie of the 20th century.

Write *true* or *false* after each statement about the reading.

1. The first Oreos were mint flavored in the middle. _____

2. Originally, Oreo was available in both lemon meringue and cream flavors. _____

3. The Oreo cookie is considered the bestselling cookie of the 20th century.

_____

4. A child invented the Oreo. _____

5. The Greek word for "mountain" is *oreo*. _____

6. The name *Oreo* might be from the French word for "gold," which is *or*. _____

Cookie Monster

Christopher is a cookie monster. He eats more cookies than any boy should. Christopher eats cookies for breakfast, cookies for lunch, and cookies for dinner. He also snacks on cookies and has them for dessert!

Christopher's mother always warns him, "Cookie Monster Christopher, you better watch out. You eat too many cookies, and bad things happen to little boys who do that!" Christopher shrugs off these warnings each and every time. This evening at dinner, he once again didn't react when his mother shook her finger at him, proclaiming, "No more cookies for you today, Christopher. You should not eat more than one cookie per day!"

Christopher went to bed with a belly full of cookies. He felt sick from all the cookies he had eaten that day, but he did not care—until morning.

Christopher woke for school and intended to take a shower, as he always did on school days. But when Christopher saw himself in the mirror, he could not believe his cookie-loving eyes. Christopher had turned into a giant chocolate chip cookie! He still had arms and legs and a head, but his whole midsection was replaced with a flat, crumbly cookie! He was a warm brown color with chocolate chunks peppered all over him.

When Christopher's mother saw him, she simply shook her head and reminded him, "I told you so!" Then, she sniffed him and said, "Mmmm, you smell delicious!" and took a nibble of him! At school, his science teacher, Ms. Shortbread, broke off a piece of Christopher's cookie body, too. During recess, Christopher's entire class surrounded him in a circle, salivating like animals. They all wanted a bite of Christopher's cookie body.

Christopher could barely fend off all the hungry people who were trying to eat him! And, with every bite, Christopher's cookie body was getting smaller and smaller. If this continued, there would be nothing left of Cookie Monster Christopher. When school ended, Christopher ran all the way home, chased by cookie-hungry classmates the whole way. He ran straight to his room, locked the door, and hid under the covers. He couldn't afford to lose one more bite of his now-tiny cookie self.

He should not have eaten so many cookies, but rather just one per day, like his mother told him. Christopher lay in bed and cried himself to sleep, promising himself that he would never eat another cookie as long as no one ate him.

The next morning, Cookie Monster Christopher opened his eyes to greet the day. He stretched and yawned and felt his dog, Oreo, licking his feet. "No, Oreo!" he shouted. Christopher had nearly forgotten that he was now a delectable treat, even to his own dog. Christopher threw the covers off and was about to run away from Oreo when he realized that he had a belly . . . and hips . . . and shoulders! Much to his relief, Christopher was no longer a cookie.

He walked downstairs for breakfast, and his mother offered him a waffle, just as she did every morning, to which he usually replied, "No, I'll have cookies, thank you." But today Christopher gleefully accepted the plate of syrupy waffles.

Answer the questions about the story.

1. What is the author's purpose for writing this story? Place a check next to it.

_____ to entertain

_____ to persuade

_____ to inform

2. Is this story a fantasy or does it take place in reality? _____

3. Name two elements of the story that tell you the answer. _____

_____

4. Place a check next to the story's genre, or type.

_____ informational

_____ fable

_____ how-to

5. Dialogue is what a character says. Underline the dialogue in paragraph 2.

6. How do you think Christopher feels at the end of the story? _____

_____

Cookie Kid

The day after Cookie Monster Christopher transformed into a cookie, he was interviewed by news stations all around the area. Everyone wanted to talk to the Cookie Kid.

Answer the reporter's questions in the way you think Cookie Monster Chistopher would.

1. Christopher, what was your first thought when you woke up as a cookie? _____

_____

_____

_____

2. How did people perceive your cookie self? _____

_____

_____

_____

3. Did it physically hurt when people bit into you? _____

_____

_____

_____

4. How did it feel to be wanted because you tasted delicious, Christopher? _____

_____

_____

5. Did you think you would ever turn back into a boy again? _____

_____

6. Finally, would you ever like to be a cookie for a day again? _____

_____

_____

Groundhogs

Groundhogs are large rodents that are also called marmots or woodchucks. Generally, groundhogs are solitary mammals, which means that they keep to themselves. Groundhogs also hibernate through the winter, sleeping away the cold, dark days, and then waking again come spring. They live in burrows in many parts of the world, including North America, Europe, and Asia.

Groundhogs have bulky bodies with short limbs, so they move fairly slowly. They have black eyes and black feet with sharp claws. Like all rodents, their incisor teeth grow throughout their lives, which is why they chew on things. Gnawing helps wear down their long teeth.

North American groundhogs are either gray or brown. They can grow to be up to two feet long and have long, bushy tails. Another type of groundhog found on the North American continent is the whistler, or hoary marmot. They are larger than North American groundhogs. They are white and gray and can be found in northwestern North America. A third type of groundhog native to North America is the yellow-bellied marmot, which is found from southwestern Canada down to New Mexico.

Groundhogs feed mostly on plants, making these rodents primarily herbivores. They eat grass, seeds, leaves, flowers, and fruit, but sometimes also eggs and insects. Groundhogs have many natural predators. They are prey to foxes, wolves, coyotes, and bobcats. But groundhogs have keen eyesight and hearing, which help them recognize when predators are approaching and they need to escape to their burrows.

Place a check next to the word or phrase that best defines each term.

1. The word *hibernate* in paragraph 1 means

_____ be active.

_____ wake up.

_____ be inactive.

2. The word *herbivore* in paragraph 4 means

_____ plant eater.

_____ meat eater.

_____ eater of anything.

3. The word *solitary* in paragraph 1 means

_____ alone.

_____ busy.

_____ social.

4. The word *gnaw* in paragraph 2 means

_____ swallow.

_____ chew.

_____ digest.

Groundhog Day

Groundhog Day falls every February 2, and it is a completely unscientific tradition that dates back many centuries. The idea that animals can predict weather has a long history.

Historians believe that Groundhog Day began with European Christians, who celebrated Candlemas Day on February 2. Candlemas Day celebrated the presentation of Christ in the Temple. If the weather was sunny on Candelmas Day, then winter would last a while longer. But if it was cloudy, they believed that winter would soon be over.

Supposedly, the Germans also began following this tradition, and that's when animals became involved. The Germans believed that if the sun made an appearance on Candlemas Day, a hedgehog would cast a shadow, thus predicting six more weeks of bad weather.

Pennsylvania's earliest settlers were Germans, and these immigrants brought this belief to the American colonies. There weren't any hedgehogs there, so they determined that the groundhog, which resembles the European hedgehog, would replace the hedgehog as a predictor of weather. Thus, the modern tradition of Groundhog Day began.

Every February 2, the groundhog leaves the burrow, where it has been hibernating all winter long. If the groundhog cannot see its shadow, it will remain above ground, ending its hibernation. This means that winter is over and spring will soon begin. However, if the sun is shining on February 2, the groundhog's shadow will be visible. The groundhog will return to its burrow to hibernate for another six weeks, because it knows that winter is not over just yet.

Unscramble the Groundhog Day terms mentioned in the reading.

1. groogundh _____

2. atweher _____

3. teheribna _____

4. nteriw _____

5. gmanser _____

6. leascandm _____

Punxsutawney Phil

The most famous groundhog in the United States is undoubtedly Punxsutawney Phil, who makes his annual weather predictions outside his burrow on Gobbler's Knob in the town of Punxsutawney, Pennsylvania. Every February 2, thousands of people gather in Punxsutawney to await Phil's verdict. According to the Groundhog Club's Inner Circle, who are a group of local dignitaries responsible for carrying on the tradition of Groundhog Day, there has been only one Punxsutawney Phil. He has been making predictions for more than 120 years and credits his long life to drinking an "elixir of life," for which the recipe is secret.

Contrary to what some may say, the Inner Circle does not make Phil's predictions for him. When Phil emerges from his burrow, he speaks to the Groundhog Club president in "Groundhogese." This is a special language only understood by the president of the Inner Circle. Phil's prediction is then translated. The Inner Circle plans all Groundhog Day events and is responsible for the care and feeding of Phil.

Punxsutawney Phil has had an illustrious career thus far. Phil was able to meet President Ronald Reagan in 1986, he appeared on the *Oprah Winfrey Show* in 1995, and in 2001, Phil's prediction was shown live on the JumboTron at Times Square in New York City. He is one busy and successful groundhog!

Answer the questions about the reading.

1. Who is Punxsutawney Phil and why is he famous? _____

_____

2. Where does he live? _____

3. What has allowed him to live for so long? _____

4. What is the Inner Circle? _____

_____

5. What language does Phil speak? _____

6. Name one special thing Phil has been able to do during his career so far. _____

_____

Déjà Vu

Claire woke for school when her alarm clock buzzed at 7:00 AM, as it always did. She went to the kitchen for breakfast and her mother greeted her, "Good morning, sweetheart. Cereal for breakfast?" Claire nodded and sat down at the table. "Are you ready for your math test?" Claire's mother asked her.

Claire looked at her mother, puzzled, and asked, "What do you mean, Mom? My math test was yesterday." Claire's mother replied, "No, honey, yesterday was Sunday. You didn't have school yesterday." Claire shook her head and thought, *I must be really groggy*.

Claire went to school, and during the whole day she felt like she had already seen and done the things that were happening to her. The problems on her math test looked really familiar, and she was certain the cafeteria had just offered the identical lunch menu the day before. *But yesterday was Sunday*, she reminded herself.

The next day, Claire woke for school when her alarm clock buzzed at 7:00 AM, as it always did. She went to the kitchen for breakfast and her mother greeted her, "Good morning, sweetheart. Cereal for breakfast?" Claire nodded and sat down at the table. "Are you ready for your math test?" Claire's mother asked her.

Claire's eyes grew wide and she slowly turned to stare at her mother. She was utterly confused. "Mom, my math test was *yesterday*," Claire said with suspicion. Claire's mother replied, "No, honey, yesterday was Sunday. You didn't have school yesterday." Claire shot up straight in her chair, and said, "What did you just say?" Claire's mother repeated, "No, honey, yesterday was Sunday. You didn't have school yesterday." *What on earth is going on?* Claire wondered.

She went to school to see how the rest of the day proceeded. She was surprised (but not completely surprised!) that the problems on her math test looked really familiar, and she was certain the cafeteria had just offered the identical lunch menu the day before. *I'm even having the same thoughts!* Claire realized.

At dinner, Claire's mother announced, "Guess what I'm making for supper tonight . . . " To which Claire replied, "Let me think on that . . . umm, spaghetti and meatballs?" Claire's mother answered, "That's right! How'd you know?" "Just a lucky guess," Claire explained. But, of course, Claire's mother had made spaghetti and meatballs for dinner the night before.

She went to bed that night thinking, *Everything will be normal in the morning*. Claire woke for school when her alarm clock buzzed at 7:00 AM, as it always did. She went to the kitchen for breakfast and her mother greeted her, "Good morning, sweetheart. Cereal for breakfast?" Claire nodded and sat down at the table. "Are you ready for your math test?" Claire's mother asked her. Claire realized that it was not just déjà vu that she was experiencing. She was reliving the same day of her life over and over again!

That's when Claire decided that if she were going to change her life back to normal, she would have to shake things up. "I'll have a smoothie for breakfast this morning, Mom," she chirped. *Let's see how this goes*, she thought.

Answer the questions about the story.

1. Which sentence in paragraph 2 tells you that something strange is happening to Claire? Underline it.

2. Circle a part of paragraph 3 that reinforces this.

3. What happens in paragraph 4? _____

_____

4. How does Claire feel about this? Underline it.

5. When Claire pondered what was happening to her, what thought did she have? _____

_____

6. How did Claire know what was for dinner? Underline the sentence.

7. How did Claire's third day start off? _____

_____

8. Which sentence in the last paragraph tells you how Claire plans to deal with her strange problem? Underline it.

Vivaldi and Bach

 Antonio Vivaldi (1678-1741) is known as the most influential composer and violinist of his time. Born in Italy, Vivaldi was known as the Red Priest because he was a priest and he had red hair.

Vivaldi is perhaps best known for his concertos called *The Four Seasons*, but he wrote nearly 500 concertos in total. His father, who was also a talented musician, trained him. In 1703, Vivaldi was ordained, or became, a priest, and in the same year he began teaching musically talented orphans.

After 1713, Vivaldi was active as an opera composer and producer in Venice. He traveled to other cities to oversee performances of his operas. Sadly, Vivaldi died in poverty in Vienna in 1741. But his contributions to music were significant.

One musician on whom Vivaldi had a considerable influence was named Johann Sebastian Bach. To this day, Bach is hailed as one of the world's greatest musical geniuses.

Bach was born on March 21, 1685, in Eisenach, Germany. He came from musical heritage. Over seven generations, his family produced more than 50 prominent musicians.

Around 1712, Bach encountered the instrumental concertos of Antonio Vivaldi. Hearing these works had a major impact on Bach's own musical style. He created keyboard arrangements of works by Vivaldi and other great Italian composers. This improved his skills and helped him become a masterful organist and composer.

Bach was known as an impossibly creative man with endless amounts of energy. He composed an enormous amount of material—more than 1,000 pieces—including works for the organ, violin, clavichord, harpsichord, chamber orchestra, and human voice. Bach worked at a number of German courts as an organist or music director, and he spent the final 27 years of his life in Leipzig, teaching and composing.

Which musician is described? Write *V* for Vivaldi or *B* for Bach next to each statement.

1. _____ His family produced more than 50 prominent musicians.

2. _____ He was born in Italy and known as the Red Priest.

3. _____ He is best known for his concertos called *The Four Seasons*.

4. _____ He composed an enormous amount of material—more than 1,000 pieces.

5. _____ He was known as an impossibly creative man with endless amounts of energy.

Duke Ellington

Duke Ellington is considered the greatest composer in the history of jazz music and one of the greatest musicians of the 20th century. Duke led an orchestra, played piano, and composed more than 2,000 pieces of music.

Duke's real name was Edward Kennedy Ellington, but a classmate gave him the nickname Duke. Duke started taking piano lessons when he was in elementary school, but he hated them. He picked them up again when he was a teenager.

Duke wanted to emulate ragtime pianist Harvey Brooks, whom he had seen perform. Duke loved that Brooks played the piano in a free and expressive manner—not in a way that followed the rules of classical piano. So Duke practiced playing piano so much, and his fingers moved so fast, that his fingers started to seem like they were flying over the keys! He even learned to arrange melodies as he played.

By the time Duke Ellington was 19, he started playing at parties, dance halls, and other venues. In 1923, he left his hometown of Washington, D.C., and moved to New York City to play in different jazz clubs and dance halls there. Duke got a job playing at the famous Harlem jazz club known as the Cotton Club, and he began to produce sophisticated arrangements of his own. Duke Ellington and his orchestra played at the Cotton Club for eleven years. They became extremely popular, and Duke toured the world, playing with his orchestra and composing thousands of songs.

Duke also composed ballets, musicals, film scores, and more. By 1969, Duke Ellington had become one of the most respected musicians and composers in the world.

Answer the questions about the reading.

1. What musician did Duke Ellington want to emulate? _____

2. What was the name of the jazz club in New York City where Duke played? _____

_____

3. How many pieces of music did Duke Ellington compose? _____

4. How did Duke feel about piano lessons when he was a child? _____

5. Where is Duke Ellington originally from? _____

If I Were a Rock Star

As you read the story, fill in each blank with any word from the correct part of speech. Have fun!

If I were a _____ rock star, I'd eat _____ for
ADJECTIVE   TYPE OF FOOD

breakfast every day. If I were a rock star, I'd have _____ people
NUMBER

_____ for me—just because I could. If I were a rock star, I'd hire a
VERB ENDING IN "ING"

_____ to do things like massage my _____ and feed
NOUN   PART OF THE BODY

my _____. If I were a rock star, I'd _____ in a private
ANIMAL   VERB

jet to my private island in _____. If I were a rock star, maybe I'd get to
COUNTRY

meet _____, the _____ of the United States. I'd
PERSON IN ROOM   OCCUPATION

_____ in a _____ mobile all over town and I'd wear
VERB   SILLY WORD

a new _____ every day of the week.
ARTICLE OF CLOTHING

Noted

An orchestra would face difficulty in making music together if each player did not know how long to hold each note. Each instrument would start its own beat or melody, and nothing would come together properly. This is why it is so important for a musician to know what each note looks like and how long it is supposed to be held.

Below is a chart of the most common types of musical notes. The chart tells how many beats per measure each note should be held. The length of a measure is determined by the time signature at the beginning of a piece of music.

whole note	o	4 beats per measure
half note	♩	2 beats per measure
quarter note	♩	1 beat per measure
eighth note	♪	$\frac{1}{2}$ beat per measure
sixteenth note	♬	$\frac{1}{4}$ beat per measure

Answer the questions about the chart.

1. Which note lasts for $\frac{1}{2}$ beat per measure? _____

2. Which note resembles a circle? _____

3. For how many beats does a sixteenth note last? _____

4. Which note has two flags? _____

5. Which note lasts longer, a whole note or a half note? _____

6. How does a quarter note look different from a half note? _____

_____

The King

Elvis Presley, also known as The King of Rock 'n' Roll, was born on January 8, 1935, in Tupelo, Mississippi. He was a rock 'n' roll musician, an actor, and, most importantly, a cultural icon—to the extent that he is known worldwide by his first name alone.

 As Elvis grew up, he was influenced by many types of music: He heard the pop and country music of the time, gospel music in church, and R&B on historic Beale Street in Memphis, Tennessee. In 1954, Elvis Presley began his singing career, and within two years he was an international sensation. His sound and style was a unique combination of his diverse musical influences. He rocked out and danced to music in a way no one had seen before, and he was handsome, too! Elvis ushered in a whole new era of American music and popular culture.

During the course of his remarkable career, Elvis appeared on many television shows and specials, and he performed live concerts on tour and in Las Vegas. Elvis has sold more records than any other artist in the world—more than one billion. He also starred in 33 successful movies. Elvis won three Grammy awards, and he was also awarded a Grammy Lifetime Achievement Award. Elvis even famously served in the U.S. Army!

Elvis lived in Graceland, a now-famous mansion in Memphis, Tennessee. He died at his estate on August 16, 1977. It is now a national landmark and museum open to the public, so that fans can continue to worship The King of Rock 'n' Roll.

Answer the questions about the reading.

1. Elvis was born when and where? _____

2. What types of music influenced Elvis? _____

_____

3. What were two of the significant achievements of his life? _____

_____

4. What is Elvis's home named? _____

5. What is Elvis's nickname? _____

Rock 'n' Roll Camp

Charlotte excitedly settled into her bunk and met her roommates, Jessica and Miley. The two had attended Rock 'n' Roll Camp before, and they were feverishly telling Charlotte all about what to expect during the course of the summer.

"Today, we'll go to opening ceremonies and play some meet-and-greet games. Then, later, there will be a campfire with an open mic, so anyone and everyone is encouraged to perform!"

Charlotte looked down at the floor. "What's wrong—you don't like open mic nights?" asked Miley. "Um, well, I, um, just don't like performing in front of large groups is all," Charlotte stammered. Jessica stepped in. "Oh, I have the perfect cure for that. I used to have stage fright, too, and then someone recommended that when I walk up there, I just imagine that the entire audience is in their underwear. It's hard not to feel comfortable if you're the only person with clothes on!" Charlotte nodded.

That night, Charlotte watched anxiously as camper after camper performed fireside. Finally, it was Charlotte's turn. Her breath became shallow and she felt a lump well up in her throat. But she stood up and approached the microphone. She remembered what Jessica had told her earlier that day. She almost laughed aloud when she envisioned the camp director and her new bunkmates all in their underwear!

When Charlotte opened her eyes again, she pulled her guitar toward her torso, bent the microphone down to her mouth, and began to play. It was definitely easier to play for people in their underwear!

Answer the questions about the story.

1. What problem does Charlotte have in the story? _____

_____

2. How does a friend suggest that she solve her problem? _____

_____

3. How do you think Charlotte might feel the next time she has to perform in front of a large crowd? _____

4. Have you ever been afraid to speak or perform in front of others? Explain. _____

_____

Run-DMC

 Run-DMC was an early, influential rap group from New York City. Run-DMC was composed of three friends: Joseph "Run" Simmons, Darryl "DMC" McDaniels, and Jason "Jam Master Jay" Mizell. The trio changed the face of modern music.

Run-DMC used spoken rhymes, or raps, on top of strong beats to create their music. In the early 1980s, this was a new and unusual sound. Run-DMC also incorporated elements of rock music into their sound. This helped popularize rap—which had been enjoyed mainly by black people—among many white listeners. Run-DMC also played a large role in creating rap fashion. They wore warm-up suits, gold jewelry, and their hallmark Adidas sneakers.

Run-DMC released its first album in 1984, using only a drum machine and the DJ's record turntable noises for accompaniment. The album was a hit. Rap music was on the rise, and Run-DMC was leading the charge.

But by 1985, a number of violent incidents at rap concerts caused the media to focus negatively on rap, accusing that music culture of encouraging violence and drug abuse. However, Run-DMC and other rap and hip-hop groups carried on through the 1980s and 1990s, and today rap is one of the most popular and critically successful genres. Among their many achievements, Run-DMC were the first rappers to achieve mainstream success, be regularly broadcast on MTV, and appear on the television program *American Bandstand*.

Answer the questions about the reading. Write the letter of the answer on the line.

1. Which term best describes this type of reading? _____

    a. how-to

    b. fiction

    c. biography

2. Which term best describes the members of Run-DMC? _____

    a. pioneers

    b. followers

    c. drones

3. Which term best describes their style of music at the time? _____

    a. common

    b. innovative

    c. typical

4. Which term best describes the image of rap by 1985? _____

    a. unflattering

    b. moral

    c. righteous

Singing Sensation

Write a story about what you think is happening in the picture. Use the title to guide you.

_____

_____

_____

_____

_____

_____

_____

_____

_____

_____

_____

Reading Music

Music is written as what is known as sheet music. Upon first glance, sheet music may look incredibly complicated, but it is really quite simple to read.

First, the staff is the series of five lines and the four spaces between. One note is assigned to each space and each line. The staff also contains many other symbols that instruct the musician on how the piece of music should be played or sung. Below is a blank staff.

A musical note represents the pitch, or how "high" or "low" the instrument sounds, in any given moment during a piece of music. Notes are assigned a letter name from A through G. The next note after G is A, and the series begins again. Notes from A to A represent one whole octave, as do all the notes between one B and the next B, one C and the next C, and so on. Octaves can move up or down, and most singers can sing two, three, or four octaves comfortably.

To the left of the notes is a clef. It lets the musician know which octave to play the notes in, as well as what notes will be played. There are two types of clefs: a treble clef and a bass clef, and each has its own set of notes.

A treble clef is used for higher musical voices, including soprano, mezzo-soprano, alto, and tenor. It is also used for the higher-pitched musical instruments such as the alto clarinet, the B-Flat clarinet, the flute, the trumpet, and the oboe. Below is a staff with a treble clef and its notes.

The notes for the treble clef can be remembered by using the following acronyms: The lines read *Every Good Boy Does Fine*, or E G B D F. The spaces read *face*, or F A C E.

By contrast, a bass clef is used for bass and baritone voices and lower-pitched musical instruments, such as the tuba, trombone, and sousaphone. Notes for these instruments would have to sit very low beneath the treble clef staff, making them hard for players to read. So the bass clef allows them to have a different staff that they can easily read. On the facing page is a staff with a bass clef and its notes.

The notes for the bass clef can be remembered by using the following acronyms: The lines read *Good Boys Do Fine Always*, or G B D F A. The spaces read *All Cows Eat Grass*, or A C E G.

Answer the questions about the reading.

1. How many lines and spaces appear on a musical staff? _____

_____

2. What does a musical note represent? _____

_____

3. What is an octave? _____

_____

4. What is a clef? _____

_____

5. What is the difference between a treble clef and a bass clef? _____

_____

_____

6. Which type of clef contains notes in the order E G B D F? _____

7. Why was it necessary to have two clefs? _____

_____

_____

8. What do you think an *acronym* is? _____

_____

Musical Mark

Mark has always been a musical prodigy. Music fills his head every second of every day. He doesn't know where the music comes from, but it plays like an orchestra in his head.

From the time he was two years old, Mark could bang out a beat on a toy drum. He started drawing pictures of instruments, such as the violin. And when Mark's mother brought him to a music store, he picked up a violin and played it, although he'd never seen or touched one before. When Mark was only four years old, he began taking piano lessons, and soon surpassed the skill level of all the other students and, eventually, his instructor!

Mark can play the most complex pieces by composers such as Mozart as though he had written them himself. So that's what he started to do! Mark's keen ear for the balances of melody and harmony in music allowed him to write his own musical compositions. He says, "If I don't get it all out of my head, it feels like I'll explode!"

Mark can sing in three octaves and can play the piano, violin, cello, guitar, and saxophone. By the time Mark was in high school, he was playing alongside some of the country's finest musicians—he had long since outgrown the level of his high school orchestra. So when it was time for him to apply to colleges, it seemed only fitting that Mark should attend The Juilliard School of Music in New York City.

Use the story to make the following predictions.

1. Predict what Mark might like to do in his spare time. _____

2. Predict how Mark's parents feel about his musicality. _____

3. Predict how Mark might feel if he was told he was not allowed to compose music. _____

_____

4. Predict how Mark might do at music college. _____

5. Predict what Mark might do for a job when he is older. _____

6. Predict how you think adult musicians might feel when they meet Mark. _____

_____

Learning About Alaska

On January 3, 1959, Alaska was the forty-ninth state to become a part of the United States of America. The abbreviation for the state of Alaska is AK, and its largest city is Anchorage. Alaska is one of the least populated states in the U.S.A., having fewer than 700,000 residents. But in terms of its landmass, Alaska is the largest state, with an area of 656,425 square miles.

Use the reading and map to answer the questions.

1. What is the capital city of Alaska? _____

2. What country borders Alaska on the east? _____

3. What ocean borders Alaska on the north? _____

4. When did Alaska become a state? _____

5. How large is Alaska, compared to other states? _____

_____

6. What is the name of a mountain in Alaska? _____

The Iditarod

The Iditarod is an annual dogsled race in Alaska. The race is more than 1,150 miles long and follows a trail from Anchorage to Nome. The race starts on the first Saturday in March and takes about 10 days to complete. The winning dogsled racer wins a large cash prize.

The word *Iditarod* comes from an Athabaskan Indian word meaning "a distant place." The Iditarod is a grueling race that takes its competitors across frozen rivers, the tundra, and steep mountains. A group of hardy sled dogs pull a sled with a musher on it. The musher is the human guiding the sled. Alaskan malamutes and Siberian huskies are two of the breeds often used on mushing teams.

The Iditarod dogsled race memorializes the "Great Race of Mercy," which was a real race against time that saved lives threatened by disease in the early part of the 20th century. The Great Race of Mercy occurred in 1925, and it was certainly not a game or competition. In February of that year, a diphtheria epidemic threatened the city of Nome, Alaska. Diptheria is a contagious and potentially fatal disease. Fortunately, diphtheria is rare in modern times, because children are vaccinated against it.

But in the 1920s, diphtheria was a significant problem, especially for many of the native Inuit children of Alaska. These children had no previous contact with diphtheria, and therefore no immunity to it. Many of them fell ill, and the only way to save them was to transport medicine across Alaska. So twenty teams of mushers and more than 100 dogs attached to sleds trekked 674 miles from Nenana, near Anchorage, to Nome. They arrived in just $5\frac{1}{2}$ days and delivered the medicine to the sick children.

The lead dog of the final team to arrive in Nome was named Balto, a Siberian husky that has since become quite famous. There are statues of Balto in Anchorage and in Central Park, in New York City. There is even a movie about Balto, named after him. Sadly, Balto died on March 14, 1933, at the age of 14.

Every year a group of dogs runs through Alaska to memorialize Balto and the other amazing dogs that saved the children of Alaska. The first Iditarod race was run in 1973 on the one hundredth anniversary of the United States' purchase of Alaska from Russia.

Follow the directions.

1. On the lines below, write a summary of the first paragraph in this reading.

_____

_____

_____

_____

2. On the lines below, write a summary of the third paragraph in this reading.

_____

_____

_____

_____

3. On the lines below, write a summary of the fifth paragraph in this reading.

_____

_____

_____

_____

Country of Canada

Canada is part of the continent of North America. This huge country, which is made up of 3,855,103 square miles, borders the Atlantic Ocean, the Pacific Ocean, the Arctic Ocean, and the United States.

Capital	Canada's capital is Ottawa, in the province of Ontario.
Provinces and Territories	Canada has 10 provinces and 3 territories. The provinces are Alberta, British Columbia, Prince Edward Island, Manitoba, New Brunswick, Nova Scotia, Ontario, Quebec, Saskatchewan, and Newfoundland and Labrador. The territories are Nunavut, Northwest Territories, and Yukon.
Climate	Southwest Canada has a mild climate. Cold winters characterize most of the rest of Canada.
Mountains	Parts of Canada are very mountainous. The tallest mountain in Canada is Mount Logan, which is 19,850 feet tall. Canada's mountain ranges include the Appalachians, Torngats, and Laurentians in the eastern regions; the Rocky, Coastal, and Mackenzie ranges in the western regions; and Mount St. Elias and the Pelly Mountains in the northern part of the country.
Lakes	Canada has about two million lakes, covering about 7.6% of its land. The biggest lakes are Lake Huron, Lake Great Bear, Lake Superior, Lake Great Slave, Lake Winnipeg, Lake Erie, and Lake Ontario.
Rivers	The longest river in Canada is the Mackenzie River, which is 2,635 miles long. It runs through the Northwest Territories. Other important rivers are the St. Lawrence River, the Yukon River, the Columbia River, the Nelson River, the Churchill River, and the Fraser River.

Write *true* or *false* after each statement about the reading.

1. The longest river in Canada is the Mackenzie River. _____

2. Canada is part of the continent of South America. _____

3. Mount Logan is 9,850 feet tall. _____

4. Overall, Canada has a mild climate. _____

Native People

※ We traditionally inhabited the areas near the North Pole, such as parts of Alaska and Canada and all of Greenland.

※ The common name for my people is Eskimo, although we prefer to be called Inuit.

※ My people are known for building temporary winter hunting lodges called igloos, which are made from snow and ice.

※ My people are closely connected to nature. We believe that every being has a spirit and must be treated with respect.

※ Seals are the staple winter food of my people, and one of our most valued resources.

Draw a picture of me and my world in the space provided.

How to Make an Igloo

Igloos are the temporary winter homes made by the Inuit people. But you don't have to be Inuit to make one!

First find a flat area. Stamp it down with your feet. Then have an adult help you cut blocks of snow and ice out of the area.

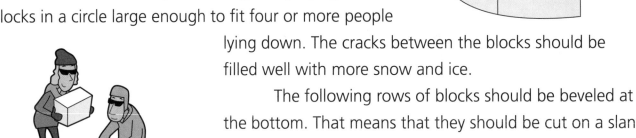

Make the base layer of the igloo by laying the blocks in a circle large enough to fit four or more people lying down. The cracks between the blocks should be filled well with more snow and ice.

The following rows of blocks should be beveled at the bottom. That means that they should be cut on a slant so the second layer begins to lean toward the middle. At first, the blocks may fall forward, so ask a second person inside to prevent the blocks from falling. After three or so blocks are placed side by side, they should hold themselves up.

Continue to work upward so that the height of the igloo is about as high as the shoulders of the person working inside.

At the top of the igloo will be a hole that can be filled with one single block. After

the outer igloo is completed, you will need to dig an entrance through the ground approaching it. Dig down and over toward the igloo.

Once you have reached the igloo chamber, dig up and into the igloo. Then, for air circulation, cut one or two vents in the blocks.

Number the igloo-making steps in the correct order.

_____ Make the base layer of the igloo by laying the blocks in a circle large enough to fit four or more people lying down.

_____ For air circulation, cut one or two vents in the blocks.

_____ The following rows of blocks should be beveled at the bottom.

_____ Start with a base area that you have stamped down with your feet.

_____ Once you have reached the igloo chamber, dig up and into the igloo.

_____ Have an adult help you cut blocks of snow and ice.

_____ After the outer igloo is completed, dig an entrance through the ground approaching it. Dig down and over toward it.

_____ Continue to work upward so that the height of the igloo is about as high as the shoulders of the person working inside.

Summer in the City

It was the middle of the summer, and the heat radiated off the city streets in waves. Jemma approached the fire hydrant and opened its floodgates, shooting water up and out into the street with great might. Suddenly, the street came to life.

Jemma's neighbors poured outside, welcoming the cool water by removing their shoes and pointing their feet into the spray. Soon enough, they were so relieved by the feeling of coolness that they threw caution to the wind and let their entire bodies be soaked.

The other children in the neighborhood played gleefully in the hydrant flow, jumping and running back and forth through it. The older residents looked on from their stoops, recalling days when they still felt up to running and playing in the street.

After they had cooled sufficiently, Jemma and the other children engaged in a game of stickball in the street, which had been blocked off by neighbors' cars. There would be no traffic to trouble the kids today. They needed their playtime—their freedom.

The hydrant served as first base, so making a hit and running to base also offered another chilling bath to help fade away the July heat. Jemma hit a line drive and darted back to the hydrant, swaying back and forth to direct the stream toward her little brother, Malcolm. He squealed in delight as he got drenched all over again.

As the sun set, casting shadows on the street, Jemma's mother came home from work and summoned her children into the apartment for supper. Jemma said farewell to her perfect summer day and ran inside, dripping all the way up the stairwell.

Answer the questions about the story.

1. Describe the setting in this story. _____

2. Who is the protagonist, or main character, of this story? _____

3. Describe one thing that the main character feels. _____

_____

4. Describe one thing that the main character hears. _____

_____

World's Largest Cities

CITY	COUNTRY	POPULATION
Tokyo	Japan	33,200,000
New York City	United States	18,900,000
Sao Paulo	Brazil	17,800,000
Mexico City	Mexico	17,700,000
Osaka-Kobe	Japan	16,425,000
Mumbai	India	16,368,000
Manila	Philippines	9,932,000
Seoul	South Korea	9,800,000
Jakarta	Indonesia	8,389,000
Lagos	Nigeria	5,200,000

Use the chart to answer the questions.

1. In what country is the most populated city in the world? _____

2. Which city has a population of 16,368,000? _____

3. Which country boasts 2 of the 10 largest cities in the world? _____

4. In what country is Manila? _____

5. What is the population of Mexico City? _____

6. What is the second largest city in the world? _____

Higgins in the City

Higgins was lost. And Higgins was lost in one of the largest, most overwhelming places in the world: New York City. Higgins trotted down the sidewalk, darting in and out of legs and feet to avoid all the pedestrians. They were far too busy to notice a lost, little dog.

Higgins came upon a playground, which resembled ones at home in the country. Higgins would normally avoid the loud confusion of a playground, but many hours had passed since he had gotten lost, and he was ravenously hungry. Higgins sniffed around, hoping to find the spare crumbs of cookies and pretzels dropped by the children. But his hunt was short, for before him sat a squirrel, offering a nut. "Take this," the squirrel told Higgins. "You're lost, I'm guessing."

"Well, yes," Higgins responded, "I was frightened by a car horn and I ran from my owner, and now I can't find her again."

"Where are you staying?" asked the squirrel.

"Um, I think it's a hotel…called the Chandler. Yes, the Chandler—that's it."

"I don't know it, but let's ask my buddy if he knows where that hotel is. We'll get you back there, have no worries," the kind squirrel reassured him. Higgins followed the squirrel out of the playground and into a large, open area, where city folk were walking and riding bikes and reading books in the grass.

"Hey, Clyde! Where's the Chandler hotel?" the squirrel asked a pigeon, who was standing among a hundred pigeons, all looking identical. "Oh, hey squirrel! What, do we have another lost country dog today?" Clyde the pigeon asked the squirrel, his eyes scanning little lost Higgins. "Yup!" the squirrel answered. "Can you guys take care of him?" "Sure!" Clyde said enthusiastically, "C'mon flock! We're taking this lost dog down to the West 30s and Park!"

Suddenly, the pigeons circled poor Higgins, moving closer and closer toward him. Then, they all began grabbing at his fur with their beaks! Higgins scarcely knew how to react, and before he knew it, he felt himself being lifted off the ground. He rose slowly, but steadily. The pigeons were going to carry him back to his owner!

As Higgins and the pigeons soared over the Big Apple, Higgins got a bird's-eye view (literally!) of its splendor. He saw the entire Central Park. He saw the Hudson River on one side and the East River on the other. And just as the Empire State Building came into sight, the pigeons began their descent toward the ground. They placed Higgins on a doorstep in front of a grand hotel with a doorman confusedly watching.

Then, just as quickly as they had picked him up, the pigeons flew away again, calling down to Higgins, "Hope you enjoy your stay in New York City!" Higgins shook his fur and looked around. He heard a squeal and recognized the unmistakable voice of his owner. She burst through the glass doors of the hotel and scooped little Higgins off the doorstep. Higgins was home again.

Answer the questions about the story.

1. Who is the protagonist of this story? _____

2. What is the conflict in this story? _____

_____

3. How do you think he feels about this problem? _____

_____

4. What parts of this story do you feel are based in reality? What parts are based in fantasy?

_____

_____

_____

5. Name one secondary character in this story. _____

6. What do you think the last line of the story means? _____

_____

Brain Matters

The human brain has three main parts: the cerebrum, the cerebellum, and the brain stem. The cerebrum is the largest part of the brain. It makes up about 85% of the total weight of the brain, and it looks like a large, pinkish-gray walnut. The cerebrum controls most of your intelligent functions, such as thinking and speaking. It is divided into halves, called the cerebral hemispheres.

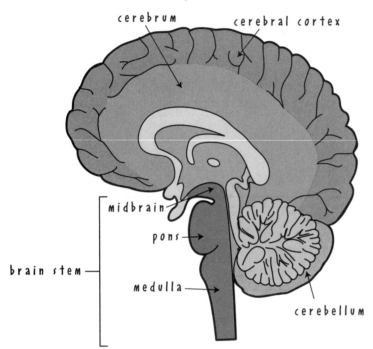

The cerebral cortex is the outside layer of the cerebrum. The "wrinkles" on the brain are the bumps and grooves on the cerebral cortex. Because of its grayish-brown color, scientists call this part of the brain "gray matter." Deep inside the cerebrum are a group of structures called the basal ganglia. These areas are important for controlling movement. The amygdala is another part of the cerebrum. It is important for memory and emotional behavior. Another structure within the cerebrum is the hippocampus. It is important for transferring memories from short-term memory to long-term memory.

The cerebellum is the second main part of the human brain. It is located at the back of the skull. It is about the size of a golf ball and is shaped like cauliflower. The cerebellum coordinates your movements and motions. It controls your reflexes and your sense of balance.

The brain stem is the third major part of the brain. The brain stem itself has three main parts: the midbrain, the pons, and the medulla. The midbrain lies between the cerebrum and the cerebellum. It is involved in hearing and sight reflexes. Some parts of the midbrain are involved with feeling pain and moving. The pons is a bulge in the brain stem between the midbrain and the medulla. It is responsible for putting your body into the stage of sleep during which you dream. The medulla sits at the base of the brain. It is almost a continuation of the spinal cord and regulates functions such as heart rate, breathing, digestion, sleeping, and waking.

Match each part of the human brain to its characteristic.

cerebellum

It makes up about 85% of the total weight of the brain.

medulla

It is responsible for putting your body into the stage of sleep during which you dream.

cerebral cortex

It has three main parts: the midbrain, the pons, and the medulla.

cerebrum

Scientists call this part of the brain "gray matter."

pons

It sits at the base of the brain.

midbrain

It is about the size of a golf ball and is shaped like cauliflower.

brain stem

It is involved in hearing and sight reflexes.

Phineas Gage

One of the most famous patients to have received a brain injury is Phineas Gage. He has become a historical phenomenon, not only because his injury was bizarre and severe, but because it taught the scientific community a great deal about the anatomy of the human brain.

On September 13, 1848, Phineas Gage was working at his job as the foreman of a railway construction gang. While on the job site, an accidental explosion sent a tamping iron through the air. The long, pointed, metal tool measured 3 feet and 7 inches long and weighed $13\frac{1}{2}$ pounds. It was $1\frac{1}{4}$ inches in diameter at one end and tapered down to a diameter of $\frac{1}{4}$ inch at the other end. The force of the explosion drove the iron rod at high speed into Gage's left cheekbone, through his skull, and out the top of his head. It landed nearly 300 feet away.

Phineas was thrown to the ground, but he was not dead. He was not only alive, but also alert and rational within a few minutes of the accident. Phineas was taken to a nearby hotel and the local doctor, Dr. John Harlow, was called. It was reported that Phineas was sitting upright and talking, waiting for a doctor to arrive, even though there was a massive hole in his head, exposing his brain.

When Dr. Harlow examined him, Phineas was still conscious and able to answer questions about his accident. Dr. Harlow treated the wound and several months later, Phineas Gage was able to return home. It seemed a miracle that not only had Phineas survived the accident, but that his brain was unaffected by the damage. At the time it was not apparent that Phineas Gage had indeed lost something crucial in the accident: his personality.

During the next few months, Phineas's personality underwent a dramatic shift. He had been known as a polite, caring, responsible, and trustworthy man. But he was becoming a much different person. Phineas suddenly had no respect for social graces and he often lied. He was now erratic and unreliable. He often made choices against his own best interests. Phineas was no longer able to form and carry out plans. He was becoming unrecognizable to friends, family, and coworkers. Eventually, his unpredictable and unusual behavior cost him his job. He was fired from the railroad company and never worked at the level of a foreman again.

It became clear to doctors that Phineas's personality changes were a result of the accident. His brain had, in fact, been permanently damaged. They began to understand that certain portions of the brain—the areas damaged by the tamping iron—were responsible for different parts of personality.

This phenomenon showed that observing social convention, behaving ethically, and making good life choices required knowledge of strategies and rules that are separate from those necessary for basic memory, motor, and speech processing. Phineas demonstrated that there are systems in the brain dedicated primarily to reasoning. This was the reason why it was said that Phineas was "No longer Gage."

The search to find these specific brain areas has stretched from Phineas's time right up to the present day. Scientists grow ever closer to figuring out the nuances of the human brain.

Answer the questions about the reading.

1. Who was Phineas Gage and what happened to him? _____

_____

_____

2. How did you feel when you read that Phineas Gage survived? _____

_____

3. What was the immediate effect of this incident? _____

_____

_____

4. What was a later effect of this incident? _____

_____

_____

5. Name one thing that doctors learned from Phineas Gage. _____

_____

Sensible

The human body has five main senses: sight, smell, taste, hearing, and touch. Each of these senses gathers information from the environment and produces nerve signals that carry this information to the brain. Here is how they do it.

When light enters your eye, cells called rods and cones change the light into a signal, which then goes to your brain. These signals tell your brain about everything you see. There are about 120 million rods in your eyes, and they are responsible for seeing black and white. There are about 6 million cones in your eyes, and they are responsible for seeing color. The rods and cones also tell your brain about shadow, depth, and movement. Your brain combines all this data to create one complete picture.

When smells enter your nose, they reach a small patch of millions of olfactory cells. They have long, microscopic hairs, or cilia, sticking out from them. Odor particles in the air stick to the cilia and make the olfactory cells produce nerve signals, which eventually travel to the brain where they are recognized as smells.

The tongue and mouth are covered with about 10,000 taste buds. When you eat something, these taste buds send more than 1 million signals to your brain. They tell your brain about the specific types of tastes in your food or drink. One area senses sweetness, one area senses saltiness, a different area senses sourness, and finally, a fourth area senses bitterness.

When sound waves enter your ears, they are captured and sent to your brain through a system of small hairs and liquid. Neurons, or nerve cells, take these waves and transform them into nerve signals, which your brain can recognize as sounds.

When you touch something or something touches you, sensory nerve endings, which are located just below the skin, register pressure and temperature. These nerve endings gather information and send it to the brain. Every inch of your skin is covered in sensory nerve endings, but not all areas are as sensitive as others. Your hands have about 17,000 receptors, which make them especially sensitive.

Find six terms from the reading in the word puzzle below.

C	I	L	I	A	O	U	S	E	R
R	V	A	Q	E	I	O	A	O	E
J	S	C	R	E	E	N	W	N	C
R	R	Z	O	I	E	E	I	B	E
C	O	N	E	S	N	U	O	C	P
T	D	N	Q	E	O	R	S	U	T
E	S	C	A	O	G	O	T	R	O
B	E	L	O	U	W	N	U	S	R
R	I	I	H	M	O	S	D	O	S
D	Y	C	B	W	O	V	J	R	M
T	A	S	T	E	B	U	D	S	T

Skeletal System

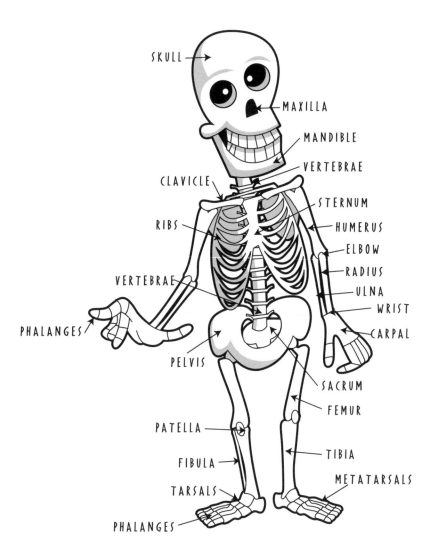

Human bones fit together to form what is known as the skeletal system, or skeleton. The skeleton supports the rest of the human body, protects the inside of the body, such as the organs, and holds it upright. When bones work together with muscles, bones also help you move.

When human beings are born, we have approximately 275 bones, but as humans grow older, many of the bones fuse together, so adults have fewer—just 206.

Interestingly, males and females have slightly different skeletons. For example, males have slightly thicker and longer legs and arms; females have a wider pelvis and a larger space within the pelvis, through which babies travel when they are born.

Use the reading and diagram to fill in the blanks.

1. The patella connects the _____ to the _____.

2. Adults have _____ bones, while babies have _____ bones.

3. Women have a wider _____ than men do.

4. The metatarsals sit between the _____ and the _____.

5. Fingers and toes are called _____.

Anatomy of an Alien

Corneus: These hefty, hornlike parts are used as a cooling system for the alien. They are also able to retract into the alien's head when not in use.

Lichems: The primary orifices through which the alien sucks the brains out of captors.

Cavitada: The internal cavity of the alien being. Typically large and swollen due to ingestion of humans.

Hoofchas: Used as secondary limbs for walking on all fours when required. Large nail-like extensions wear down during the life of the alien.

Pants: No known name in the alien world for this article, so its common human name will be used. Aliens are not known to have reproductive organs, so the purpose of these pants is unclear.

Use the diagram to answer the questions.

1. What are hoofchas? _____

2. Why is the cavitada of the alien so large? _____

_____

3. What are the lichems used for? _____

4. Why is the alien wearing pants? _____

5. Is this anatomy diagram real or fantasy? _____

6. What might be the author's purpose in creating this diagram? _____

_____

Alien Abduction

Imagine that one day you leave your home to go to school, and you encounter a spaceship right outside your door. A door in the spaceship opens, and a space alien appears and abducts you! What happens next? Write your own story. Then draw a scene from your story in the space provided.

_____

_____

_____

_____

_____

_____

_____

_____

_____

The Moon

The moon is the name used for earth's only natural satellite. After the sun, the moon is the brightest object in earth's sky. However, it shines by reflecting the light of the sun.

The moon is a slightly egg-shaped ball composed mostly of rock and metal. It has no liquid water and virtually no atmosphere, and it is lifeless. Temperatures on its surface are extreme, ranging from a maximum 260° F to a minimum of –280° F.

Here are some more facts about the moon:

Radius	1,737 km
Mass	7.35×10^{19} kg
Rotational period (time for turning on its axis)	27.32 days
Orbital period (time for turning around earth)	27.32 days
Average distance from earth	384,400 km

Complete each sentence about the reading and chart. Circle the letter of the answer.

1. The moon is earth's only natural _____.

   a. dwarf planet

   b. satellite

   c. rocket

2. The moon shines by reflecting the light of the _____.

   a. stars

   b. Earth

   c. sun

3. The moon's rotational period is _____.

   a. 27.32 days

   b. 72.32 days

   c. 37.22 days

4. The moon is _____ away from earth.

   a. 843,400 km

   b. 384,400 km

   c. 438,800 km

5. The moon has no _____.

   a. liquid water

   b. solid ground

   c. volcanoes

6. The moon is shaped like a(n) _____.

   a. egg

   b. book

   c. box

Moon Phases

As it moves along its orbit around earth, each day the moon appears differently. This change in appearance is known as lunar phases. Half of the moon is always in sunlight, and so the phase of the moon depends on how much of the sunlit half can be seen at any one time. The cycle takes about a month.

1. In the phase called the new moon, the face is completely in shadow. Draw an image of a new moon.

2. As the moon begins to grow on the right side, it is called a waxing crescent moon. Draw an image of a crescent moon.

3. About a week after the new moon, the moon is in first quarter, resembling a luminous semicircle. Draw a first-quarter moon.

4. Another week later, the full moon shows its fully lighted surface. Draw a full moon.

5. One week later, the moon is in its last quarter, and it appears as a semicircle again, but on the left side. Draw a last-quarter moon.

6. Then, it returns to a crescent form on the left side as it approaches new moon. Draw a waning crescent moon.

Big Changes

Jackson lived in a normal house, attended a normal school with normal teachers, all in a normal town. But one day, ten-year-old Jackson began to grow hair from his ears. Jackson's mom helped him pluck the hairs, and he soon forgot about them.

The following day, as Jackson was dressing for school, he noticed hairs on his chest. *Cool*, he thought. *Real men have hair on their chests, like my dad*. Later that day, as Jackson was changing his shoes for soccer practice, he was alarmed that he also had hairs growing from the top of his feet and toes. Jackson began exploring his body, and what he found was astonishing. Jackson had hair—or, more accurately, fur—growing on every inch of his body.

It grew from his arms and his neck, and from his hands and his behind! It was all over him. When Jackson looked in the mirror, he saw fur covering his face, of course. But he saw that he also had fangs!

Jackson bolted from the locker room and ran all the way home. His fur was so thick at this point that it filled up his clothes, making them tight and warm. Jackson felt as hot as if he had been playing soccer in the July heat, though he wasn't sweating at all. He was, however, panting like a dog.

When Jackson arrived home, he immediately ran into his bedroom and looked up his symptoms on the Internet. He assumed that he must have some sort of strange disease. But Jackson came across a page that made his eyes grow wide. It described the phenomenon of *loup-garou*. This made Jackson howl—literally. *Could it be?* he wondered.

Answer the questions about the story.

1. What was the first unusual thing that happened to Jackson? _____

_____

2. What shocked Jackson when he looked in the mirror? _____

3. How did Jackson feel as he ran home? _____

_____

4. What do you think is happening with Jackson? What told you? _____

_____

Moon Myths, Busted

The moon is made of cheese! The moon is not, in fact, made from cheese, although its "holey" surface does resemble Swiss cheese. The holes on the moon are called craters, and they are dents from meteors hitting the surface of the moon many years ago. There are thousands of large and small craters on the moon.

There is a Man in the Moon. When the moon is full, many people claim that they can see the man in the moon. The face they see isn't actually a man at all, but just a series of crevices and mounds that create what looks like a face.

There are creatures living on the moon. Humans have been there, and they didn't see anything alive. In fact, nothing can be alive on the moon because there is no atmosphere and no water on the moon. During the lunar day, the sunlight would burn a living thing, and in contrast, anything alive would freeze at night.

The moon disappears. The moon is always there. However, sometimes you can't see it! During the new moon, the moon and the sun are on the same side of earth. The moon appears dark, or as if it is gone. But it is merely in shadow. If the moon were to actually disappear one day, life on earth would be greatly impacted. The moon controls the ocean tides, so the tides would reduce in strength. The moon also keeps the angle between earth's rotation axis and its plane of orbit within a narrow range. This is why the seasons occur with temperate changes. Without the moon, the climate would change, and the differences between winter and summer would be greater than they are now.

Unscramble the words mentioned in the reading.

1. adshow _____

2. tdesi _____

3. atcrers _____

4. moeters _____

5. ifle _____

6. onrotati _____

7. echese _____

8. nma in hte mnoo

_____

Down Under

E-mail message   _ □ ✕

From: jesse@mymessage.com

Subject: Australia

Fontstyle ▼ 10 ▼

Hey, mate,

I'm writing to you from the land down under—Australia! People here don't really call it that, but people from other countries do because Australia sits nearly at the "bottom" of the globe.

Our trip has been excellent so far. The flight from America was almost an entire day long, so that was tough. But once we arrived, the good times started to roll! These Aussies sure know how to have fun. The people here are so welcoming and relaxed. It's different from the fast pace of America.

So far, we have gone diving on the Great Barrier Reef, which was phenomenal. I saw species of fish I hadn't seen in the Caribbean or anywhere else. I even saw a shark from a distance. Good thing he wasn't hungry—or a great white! They live in the waters around here, too, you know.

We also went to see the Opera House in Sydney. It is a magnificent architectural creation. I even saw a kangaroo! Did you know that they are marsupials? They are also sometimes shot for their meat, which makes me sad. There is a lot of controversy about it here.

I hope you're having a great time in Italy this week. See you back in the States!

Love,
Jesse

Answer the questions about the e-mail.

1. Who is the author of this e-mail? _____

2. From where is the author writing? _____

3. Why is it called the "land down under"? _____

_____

4. What animal does the author see there? _____

5. What does he learn about that animal? _____

_____

6. What is one difference the author sees between life in Australia and life in America?

_____

Colorful World

Coral reefs are rich, complex ocean habitats that develop in shallow, warm water. Coral prefer temperatures between 70°F and 85°F, and so they most often form near land and in the tropics.

Coral reefs may be found off the eastern coast of Africa, off the southern coast of India, in the Red Sea, and off the coasts of northeast and northwest Australia. The Great Barrier Reef, located off the coast of Australia, is the largest coral reef in the world. It is more than 1,257 miles long. There are also coral reefs near Polynesia, off the coast of Florida, and in the Caribbean downward toward South America.

Of the three different types of coral reefs, barrier reefs grow parallel to shorelines and are usually separated from the land by a deep lagoon. They are called barrier reefs because they form a barrier between the lagoon and the seas, impeding travel. The second type, fringing reefs, form along a coastline. They grow on the continental shelf in shallow water. Coral atolls are the third type of reef. These rings of coral grow on top of old, sunken volcanoes (yes, there are volcanoes in the ocean!).

Some of the many creatures that inhabit coral reefs include fish, jellyfish, anemones, sponges, sea stars, crustaceans, turtles, sea snakes, snails, and mollusks. But many coral reefs and their life forms are dying out. Water pollution, careless collecting of coral specimens, and sedimentation are responsible. Sedimentation occurs when silt or sand from construction projects muddies the water and blocks the light that coral reefs need to live.

Place a check next to the word that is a synonym of, or word that means the same as, the boldfaced word.

1. Coral reefs are rich, **complex** ocean habitats.

_____ basic

_____ intricate

_____ simple

2. This kind of coral reef grows **parallel** to shorelines.

_____ equidistant

_____ perpendicular

_____ above

3. Coral most often form near land and in the **tropics**.

_____ northern

_____ polar

_____ temperate

4. They form a barrier between the lagoon and the seas, **impeding** travel.

_____ freeing

_____ clearing

_____ blocking

Casting a Line

Face the target area with your body turned at a slight angle. Aim the rod tip toward the target, at about the level of your eyes. Press and hold down the reel's release button. Swiftly and smoothly, bend your arm at the elbow, raising your hand with the rod until it reaches almost eye level. When the rod is almost vertical, the practice plug will bend it back. As the rod bends, move your forearm forward with a slight wrist movement.

Next, gently sweep the rod forward, causing the rod to bend with the motion. As the rod moves in front of you and reaches an angle between 45° and 90° to your body, release your thumb from the button.

The bend in the rod casts the bobber and bait out. Congratulations: You have just made a cast! However, if the plug landed close in front of you, then you released the thumb button too late. If the plug went almost straight up, you released the thumb button too soon.

Number the line casting steps in the correct order.

_____ Swiftly and smoothly, bend your arm at the elbow, raising your hand with the rod until it reaches almost eye level.

_____ Next, gently sweep the rod forward, causing the rod to bend with the motion.

_____ As the rod moves in front of you and reaches an angle between 45° and 90° to your body, release your thumb from the button.

_____ Face the target area with your body turned at a slight angle.

_____ As the rod bends, move your forearm forward with a slight wrist movement.

_____ Press and hold down the reel's release button.

_____ Aim the rod tip toward the target, at about the level of your eyes.

What is one potential reason why a person following these instructions would **not** make a successful cast? _____

_____

Beach Prank

As you read the story, fill in each blank with any word from the correct part of speech. Have fun!

It was a _____ summer day at the seashore. My sister decided to
ADJECTIVE

_____ with the boat, even after I had told her I wanted to use it. Rather
VERB

than get _____, I got even. I let my sister _____ until she
ADVERB   VERB

was nearly out of sight. Then, I attached a _____ to my head, pulled a pair
NOUN

of _____ over my _____ and swam out after her. I was
PLURAL NOUN   PART OF THE BODY (PLURAL)

sure to stay _____ hidden, so I wouldn't blow my cover. Just as my sister
ADVERB

was about to kick up her _____ and read a _____ book,
PART OF THE BODY   ADJECTIVE

I bumped the bottom of the boat. She _____ and looked over the edge.
VERB (PAST TENSE)

That's when I swam by with a _____ fin attached to a
ANIMAL

_____. She screamed, "_____!" and fell backwards into
NOUN   EXCLAMATION

the boat. But, then my plan kind of backfired on me. I started to _____
VERB

so hard that I swallowed _____ and nearly choked. She had to
LIQUID

_____ into the water to save me. Oops!
VERB

Great Whites

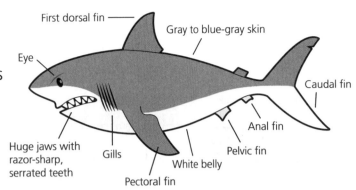

First dorsal fin

Gray to blue-gray skin

Eye

Caudal fin

Anal fin

Huge jaws with razor-sharp, serrated teeth

Gills

Pelvic fin

White belly

Pectoral fin

The great white shark is one of the most feared creatures on earth—for good reason! Great whites are massive, ferocious predators. However, most great white attacks are not fatal.

Great whites average between 12 and 16 feet long and weigh about 7,000 pounds. Some can even grow more than 21 feet long. They are gigantic! Females are larger than males, as is true for most sharks.

The great white shark has a torpedo-shaped body with a powerful, crescent-shaped tail and a pointed snout. Great whites have three main fins: the dorsal fin on its back and two pectoral fins, one on each side. When the shark is near the surface, the dorsal fin and part of the tail are visible above the water. Great whites also have five gill slits. Despite its name, most of its body is gray or blue. Only its belly is white.

The great white shark has 3,000 teeth at any one time. They are triangular, serrated, which means jagged, and up to three inches long. The first two rows of teeth are used to obtain prey; the other rows rotate into place as needed. Great whites do not chew their food. Their teeth rip prey into mouth-sized pieces that they swallow whole. Adult great whites eat larger prey, including sea lions, seals, small whales, otters, and sea turtles.

Write *fact* or *opinion* after each statement from the reading.

1. The great white shark has 3,000 teeth at any one time. _____

2. The great white shark is one of the most feared creatures on earth. _____

3. Despite its name, most of its body is gray or blue. _____

4. Great whites have three main fins: the dorsal fin on its back and two pectoral fins, one on each side. _____

5. Great whites average between 12 and 16 feet long and weigh about 7,000 pounds.

_____

6. Great whites are massive, ferocious predators. _____

Sammy's Smile

Sammy the great white shark swam silently in large circles. Marco the seahorse and his herd floated by Sammy's path. Marco slowed down to look at the pensive shark. "What's the matter, Sammy? You look glum," Marco asked. "Oh, do I?" responded Sammy the shark. "It's just that all the other sea creatures have friends that they do

things with—like you and your herd of seahorses. But no one ever wants to play with me, and I'm lonely." Marco replied, "Well, to be honest, Sammy, you're kind of intimidating to the other sea creatures."

"Intimidating? Really? But I try to be sociable. Just the other day, I swam up to Max the jellyfish and told him a joke. He darted away as soon as I said the punch line! It went like this: A group of sea creatures walks into a diner and sits down to order. The manatee says, 'I'll have the water hyacinth.' The whale says, 'I'll have the krill.' The fish says, 'I'll have the plankton.' And the great white shark says, 'I'll just have a bite of everyone else!'" With that, Sammy the shark began to laugh at his own joke, flashing 3,000 razor-sharp teeth as he did so.

Marco recoiled, but then remembered that he was being asked for friendly advice. He began, "Well, Sammy, I think your problem is twofold . . . "

Answer the questions about the story.

1. Without knowing one, what do you think great white sharks are like? _____

_____

2. Compare Sammy to what you thought about great white sharks. _____

_____

3. How would you describe Marco the seahorse? _____

4. What do you think Marco will say are Sammy's two problems? _____

_____

5. Predict what Sammy might do next. _____

_____

Roman Holiday

E-mail message _ □ ✕

From:	zoey@mymessage.com
Subject:	Italy

Fontstyle ▼ 10 ▼

Hi, Jesse,

I'm so happy to hear that you are having a good time in Australia! We are having a great time here in Italy, too. We're now in Rome, which is a city steeped in history.

We visited the magnificent Colosseum, which was a vast amphitheater used for battles. It's where the gladiators fought! Then, we went to see the Pantheon, which was used as a church beginning in the early 7th century. Did you know that the only light that enters the Pantheon comes from the opening at the dome's apex? It's also where many famous Italians are buried, including the Renaissance painter Raphael.

Finally, we went to the Vatican, which is among the most important historical sites in the world. It's the seat of the Holy Roman Catholic Church and the home of the Pope. It's where Michelangelo painted the history of creation on the ceiling of the Sistine Chapel. And did you know the Vatican is the smallest state in the world?

But perhaps the best part about Italy is the food! I've eaten my way through each city. Breads and soups and pizzas, oh my!

Ciao,
Zoey

Answer the questions about the e-mail.

1. Who is the author of this e-mail? _____

2. From where is the author writing? _____

3. Where is the e-mail's recipient? _____

4. What is one significant thing about the Vatican? _____

_____

5. What is one significant thing about the Pantheon? _____

_____

6. What do you think _ciao_ means? _____

Piece Together Pizza

Ingredients:

1 store-bought pizza crust

1 cup pizza sauce

$\frac{1}{4}$ teaspoon salt

$\frac{1}{8}$ teaspoon ground pepper

2 cups fresh mushrooms*, chopped

1 cup small broccoli florets*

$\frac{1}{2}$ cup chopped green peppers*

$\frac{1}{2}$ cup chopped green onions*

1 cup shredded mozzarella cheese

*A variety of vegetables can be chosen, depending on preference. Always have an adult help you with knives and the oven.

Directions:

1. Preheat oven to 400°F.
2. Spread sauce over crust.
3. Spread vegetables over sauce layer.
4. Sprinkle cheese on top of vegetable layer.
5. Bake for 20 to 25 minutes, or until crust is brown.

Number the recipe steps in the correct order.

_____ Bake for 20 to 25 minutes, or until crust is brown.

_____ Spread vegetables over sauce layer.

_____ Preheat oven to 400°F.

_____ Sprinkle cheese on top of vegetable layer.

_____ Spread sauce over crust.

Do you have to use the vegetables listed in the recipe? Explain. _____

_____

_____

Tasty History

Pizza has evolved into its current form very gradually. It bears the mark of many ancient cultures surrounding the Mediterranean Sea. The Greeks ate flat, round bread called *plankuntos* that was baked with an assortment of toppings. Also, Ancient Egyptians customarily celebrated the pharaoh's birthday with a flat bread seasoned with herbs.

Pizza as we know it today began developing by the 16th century, when Spaniards who had been to Mexico and Peru introduced the tomato to Italy. Prior to that time, the tomato was thought to be poisonous! The original mozzarella cheese was made from the milk of Indian water buffalo in the 7th century. It was introduced to Italy in the 18th century.

Italian and Greek peasants ate early forms of pizza for several centuries because it was an inexpensive and convenient food. But pizza eventually became popular among aristocracy. In 1889, a Neapolitan named Raffaele Esposito prepared pizza for King Umberto I and Queen Margherita, who apparently loved it. That is why a version of pizza called Pizza Margherita still exists in modern times.

The world's first true pizzeria was likely Antica Pizzeria Port'Alba, which opened in 1830 and is still in business today in Naples. Pizza made its way to the United States in 1895, when an Italian immigrant named Gennaro Lombardi opened the first U.S. pizzeria in New York City, called Lombardi's. The pizzeria is still in operation and has become a New York City tourist destination. Regardless of its origins, pizza is now consumed and enjoyed all over the world.

Answer the questions about the reading.

1. What class of people ate pizza before the 1800s? _____

2. What cultures are responsible for developing pizza? _____

_____

3. What was the first pizzeria in the United States? _____

4. Who brought the tomato to Italy? _____

5. Where did the term Pizza Margherita come from? _____

_____

African History in Brief

Africa is the world's second largest continent, covering 23 percent of earth's land area and containing 13 percent of the world's population. Africa is a land of great diversity, in terms of both culture and topography, or landscape.

Africa contains areas of lush, green forests and vast, grassy plains. It is home to barren deserts, tall mountains, and some of the mightiest rivers on earth. The people and lifestyles in Africa are equally varied. There are small villages where daily life remains largely the same as it has been for hundreds of years, and there are sprawling cities with skyscrapers and a modern economy.

Africa is the land of one of the world's first great civilizations, Ancient Egypt. But during the past 500 years, Africa has suffered greatly. European traders and colonizers sent millions of Africans to work as slaves on colonial plantations in North America, South America, and the Caribbean. By the late 19th century, European powers had seized and colonized nearly all of Africa.

By the 1960s, much of Africa had regained its independence, though reform was slow and often involved violent struggle. As a result of its long colonization, Africa emerged with a weak position in the global economy. Its communication and transportation systems were also underdeveloped, making the continent seem like a very antiquated place. Today, Africans continue to work to restore their homeland.

Use the words from the word bank to fill in the blanks.

Ancient Egypt   colonized   diversity   slaves   barren

1. Africa is a land of great _____, in terms of both culture and topography.

2. _____ arose in northeastern Africa more than 5,000 years ago.

3. Europeans sent millions of Africans to work as _____.

4. Africa is home to _____ deserts, tall mountains, and some of the mightiest rivers on earth.

5. By the late 19th century, European powers had seized and _____ nearly all of Africa.

On the Map

There are 53 different African countries. Forty-seven of these are mainland nations and the other six are surrounding island nations. Africa is commonly divided along the lines of the Sahara Desert, which cuts through the northern half of the continent. The countries north of the Sahara make up the region of North Africa, while the region south of the desert is known as sub-Saharan Africa.

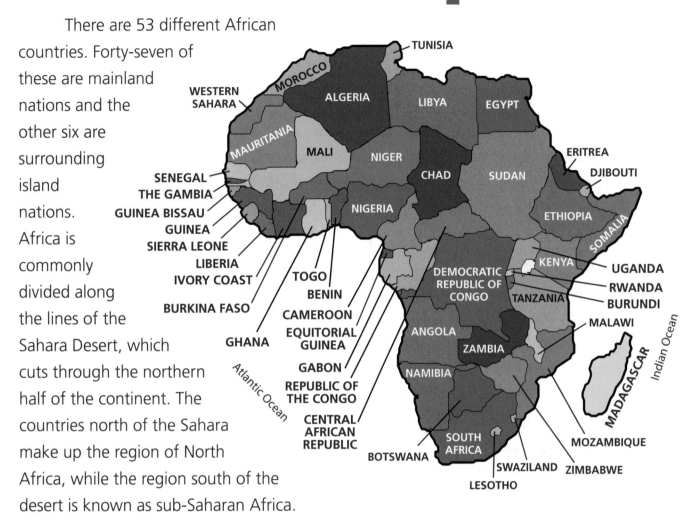

Use the map and reading to answer the questions.

1. Which ocean sits to Africa's west? Circle its name.

2. What large island sits to Africa's east? Circle its name.

3. What is the name of Africa's southernmost country? Circle its name.

4. What desert cuts through Africa? _____

5. The Darfur region is located in Sudan. Circle Sudan.

South African Adventure

We landed in the coastal city of Cape Town, the oldest port in southern Africa. It was rumored to be one of the most beautiful cities in the world—sometimes called Eden—and I have to say that I agreed.

Cape Town, South Africa, is backed by the flat-topped Table Mountain and nestled between the mountains and the sea. Cape Town has miles of pristine beaches, and I learned that the European settlers who arrived in Cape Town in 1652 are heavily responsible for influencing the city's architecture and language. Cape Town also has magnificent enclaves, or separate little villages, surrounded by oak trees.

Next, we traveled up the coastline of South Africa and inland, toward Kruger National Park. It was time to see some wildlife! Kruger National Park straddles the border of South Africa and neighboring Mozambique. Kruger is Africa's oldest wildlife sanctuary and it stretches across 6.2 million acres. That is bigger than the entire state of New Jersey.

Kruger is home to more than 500 bird and 147 mammal species, including lions, leopards, rhinos, and buffalo. We saw many of these species and the San Bushman rock paintings. We also headed to the Olifants, where we saw the majestic elephants. It was, as the locals say, *Kukahley*, or "cool!"

Answer the questions about the reading.

1. Briefly describe Cape Town. _____

_____

_____

2. Who is responsible for much of the architecture and language there? _____

_____

3. What is Kruger? _____

4. What does the author see there? _____

_____

5. What does *Kukahley* mean? _____

Nelson Mandela

Nelson Mandela dedicated his life to the struggle for racial equality in South Africa. Mandela opposed the South African system of segregation called apartheid. Today, he is one of the most famous and deeply loved leaders in the world.

Mandela was born on July 18, 1918, in Transkei, South Africa. After childhood, he became actively involved in the movement against apartheid, which is discrimination against non-Europeans in South Africa. For 20 years, Mandela led a campaign of peaceful, nonviolent defiance against the South African government and its racist policies. In 1961, he orchestrated a three-day national workers strike. He was arrested and sentenced to life imprisonment for political offenses.

Nelson Mandela spent 27 years in prison for his beliefs. When he was finally released, he resumed his fight, urging foreign powers to put more and more pressure on the South African government to reform its constitution. By 1990, his struggle came to fruition: He negotiated an end to apartheid.

In 1993, Mandela shared the Nobel Prize for Peace for his work. Then, in 1994, at the age of 77, Mandela became the first-ever democratically elected president of South Africa. He was also the country's first black president.

Mandela retired from active politics in 1999. But he remains committed to finding solutions to global problems, including AIDS.

Answer the questions about the reading. Write the letter of the answer on the line.

1. What word describes Nelson Mandela?

_____

a. lazy

b. determined

c. content

3. How do most people today feel about Nelson Mandela? _____

a. He is loathed.

b. He is feared.

c. He is respected.

2. What was apartheid? _____

a. a system of segregation

b. a water system

c. a system of economics

4. What happened to Nelson Mandela at the age of 77? _____

a. He became the first-ever democratically elected president of South Africa.

b. He died.

c. He went to prison.

Dictionary Skills

It is important for students to understand a few common conventions for dictionary use. Here is a sample entry from a dictionary:

feat \fēt\ *noun*
a remarkable, skillful, or daring action; exploit; achievement *<feats of strength>*

In this entry, the defined word, or main entry, is **feat**.

Next appears its pronunciation, usually using the phonetic alphabet: \fēt\

Then the dictionary entry indicates the word's function, or part of speech: *noun*

Next, the word is defined: a remarkable, skillful, or daring action; exploit; achievement Some words have several meanings, in which case numbers separate the varying meanings.

Then there is an example phrase or sentence that uses the defined word: *feats* of strength

Guide words are the words at the top of dictionary pages. They are usually printed in large, bold type at the upper left-hand and right-hand corner of any page. Guide words help you quickly find a word in the dictionary. The first guide word on any page tells you the first word on that page. Then, proceeding alphabetically, as dictionaries do, the second guide word indicates the last word to be found on that page.

Follow the directions.

1. Circle the words that could be found on a dictionary page between these two guide words: **peered • penetrate**

peninsula	pep	perceive	pedigree
peddling	pepper	penalties	peeking
pelican	pelted	penetrated	peddles
peeked	penthouse	penmanship	penalizes

2. Circle the words that could be found on a dictionary page between these two guide words:

massacre • masterful

massive	marshals	marshaled	marriage
masterpiece	meandered	master	massed
mathematics	masquerade	massage	massaged
mathematician	martin	massing	Maryland

3. Circle the words that could be found on a page between these two guide words:

overhauled • overloads

overeat	overcast	owned	overhearing
overruling	overweight	overdone	overlapped
overjoyed	overflow	overhead	overlapping
overdress	overloaded	overcame	overruled

Main Entry: **dog**

Pronunciation: \\'do˙g, 'däg\\

Function: *noun*

1 a: canine; *especially*: a domestic mammal (*Canis familiaris*) closely related to the gray wolf

b: a male dog; *also*: a male usually carnivorous mammal

2 a: a worthless or contemptible person **b:** fellow, chap <a lazy *dog*> <you lucky *dog*>

3 *capitalized*: either of the constellations Canis Major or Canis Minor

4 *plural*: feet

5 *plural*: ruin <going to the *dogs*>

4. What is the defined word in the entry above? _____

5. What is its function? _____

6. What is the first definition of the word? _____

_____

_____

7. What is another definition of the word? _____

_____

_____

Encyclopedia Skills

Encyclopedias are reference works that provide information on a range of subjects. They are alphabetically arranged by topic. Traditionally, encyclopedias consisted of many volumes and were housed in libraries. But today, many encyclopedias are available on CD-ROM or on the Internet, making information even easier to find.

Let's say you wanted to look up the term *jaguar*. You would first go to the J volume or section of a printed encyclopedia. Then, to get to your term quickly, you would follow guide words, just as you would when using a dictionary.

In the J volume or section, you will likely find an article about the animal called a jaguar and one about a type of car called a Jaguar. Presuming you wanted to find information about the big cat, you would be off to a good start. But additional information about the jaguar could be found elsewhere in the encyclopedia.

Remember to look through the index of an encyclopedia to access *all* of the information about a given topic. An index is a separate volume, or may appear at the back of a single volume. It contains keywords that help a person sort out all the topics covered. You might find out that there is jaguar information in the R volume under the "rain forest" section or in the C volume under "cats."

Find six terms from the reading in the word puzzle below.

I	N	D	E	X	O	I	S	E	R
N	V	A	G	E	I	N	A	O	Z
T	S	C	U	E	E	F	W	N	C
E	R	Z	I	I	E	O	I	B	E
R	O	N	D	S	N	R	O	C	P
N	D	N	E	E	O	M	S	V	T
E	S	C	W	O	G	A	T	O	O
T	E	L	O	U	W	T	U	L	R
R	I	I	R	M	O	I	D	U	S
D	Y	C	D	W	O	O	J	M	M
R	E	F	E	R	E	N	C	E	T

The Best Word

As you read the story, create a more interesting one by using a thesaurus to find a synonym for each of the words in parentheses. Be sure that the words you choose are in the correct part of speech and make sense in the story.

Theo was a (cute), affectionate little puppy. But he was also a (naughty) little puppy. Theo stole (food) from the table and knocked over the (trash) can. Theo (ate) a shoe and he refused to be housetrained. Theo's owners felt (bad). They were (worried), which meant only one thing for Theo: puppy school. At puppy school, Theo (ran) after a butterfly and (played) in the dirt. He was just as (naughty) as ever.

Rewrite the story here.

_____

_____

_____

_____

_____

_____

_____

_____

_____

Jean Craighead George

Jean Craighead George began writing in the third grade, and she hasn't stopped since. She has written more than 100 books. Most of her books involve the natural world. Jean was always drawn to the outdoors. As a child, she liked to fish, play softball, swim, catch frogs, and ride around in hay wagons with her brothers.

Jean Craighead was born on July 2, 1919, in Washington, D.C., and later attended Pennsylvania State University, where she earned degrees in science and literature. After college, she was a reporter for the *Washington Post* newspaper and for the White House Press Corps.

At first, Jean wrote books with her husband. The first one, *Vulpes, the Red Fox*, was published in 1948. The two wrote this and several more animal biographies together. They based the books on real-life experiences they had with animals they took in from the wild and kept as pets. Their writing partnership was very successful. In fact, they even won an award for best nature writing for their book *Dipper of Copper Creek*.

In 1959, *My Side of the Mountain* was published. This is one of Jean Craighead George's best-known books. It is a survival story about a boy named Sam Gribley. She based the story on her childhood and her experiences with her father and twin brothers. It was written as her own children napped and slept at night. *My Side of the Mountain* was popular with critics, parents, and teachers.

She traveled across America with her children, taking them to places where they could study animals and plants. They climbed mountains together, hiked deserts, and canoed on rivers. Her observations on these trips became material for her books.

After a trip to Alaska in 1970 with her youngest child, Jean returned home and wrote *Julie of the Wolves*. It is the story of a brave Inuit girl who gets lost on the Alaskan tundra while running away from home. The heroine forms a close bond with wild wolves. They help her to survive. The book was published in 1972, and in 1973 it received the John Newbery Medal. This honor is given to the author of the most distinguished piece of children's literature from the previous year. Just a few years after it was published, *Julie of the Wolves* was picked by the Children's Literature Association as one of the ten best American children's books of the past 200 years.

Jean Craighead George lives in Chappaqua, New York. She still writes books and is actively involved in trying to get new environmental protection bills passed through Congress.

Answer the questions about the reading.

1. What did Jean Craighead George like to do as a child? _____

_____

_____

2. What did she do before she was a book author? _____

_____

_____

3. What was her first book? _____

4. For which book did Jean Craighead George receive the Newbery medal? _____

_____

5. How did she get the idea for this book? _____

_____

6. If Jean Craighead George found an abandoned dog, what do you think she would do?

_____

_____

A New Home

Yesterday morning, I was curled up in a ball near the inside wall of a barn, freezing and hungry. I don't know why my owner left me there. That's when another human saw me shivering and came over. She rubbed my ears and spoke to me in a soothing voice, so I let her take me. Anything would have been better than staying out there in the cold.

The kind woman brought me to a place where there were many other dogs. They were all saying things like, "Welcome to the club!" and "Bring me home!" I was handed to a man, who placed me in a large box with a wire door. It wasn't so bad, though. It was warm, and there was soft bedding and water. The dog in the box next to me explained that I was at the shelter, and that no one would hurt me.

The following morning, I awoke to the sounds of the other dogs barking, "They are looking to adopt! There's a kid with them!" Then, I watched as two large humans and one small human walked slowly down the corridor. They peered into each wire box as they walked. The child bent down in front of my door and shoved his fingers through one of the holes. I sniffed him, and found that he smelled of bacon. So I licked his hand. He giggled and withdrew his hand.

 A short time later, I was allowed to step out toward him and the other humans. The child really did smell delicious, so I sniffed his ears and face and licked his nose. He giggled again. He petted my ears and belly, and by the end of the day, I was asleep beside him in a warm, fluffy bed in a cozy house. He calls me Max.

Answer the questions about the story.

1. What happened to the dog at the beginning of the story? _____

_____

2. Where does he go next? _____

3. Who does the dog meet on the following morning? _____

_____

4. Where is the dog by the end of the story, and how do you think he feels about this place? _____

_____

Saved

You might think of the SPCA or ASPCA simply as a place to adopt a cat or dog. But the first Society for the Prevention of Cruelty to Animals (SPCA) was organized to protect horses.

The SPCA dates back to 1824. It was created in England chiefly to stop the abuse of carriage horses. At the time, horses were the main form of transportation, and they suffered from bad treatment. Carriage horses were driven through awful weather conditions often with little food, water, or rest. The carriage drivers would often beat the horses if they refused to or were unable to pull the carriages. So the SPCA helped pass laws that regulated the carriage horse business.

Eventually, the SPCA expanded to include dogs and other animals in its fight against animal cruelty. In 1866, the SPCA made its way to the Western hemisphere. Known as the American Society for the Prevention of Cruelty to Animals (ASPCA), it first opened in New York City. There are now SPCAs all over the United States and the world.

Today, the mission of the SPCA is to alleviate injustices faced by animals. They do this partly by teaching and encouraging good pet parenting practices.

Answer the questions about the reading. Circle the letter of the answer.

1. The author's purpose in writing this passage is _____.

   a. to inform

   b. to persuade

   c. to entertain

2. The word *cruelty* in paragraph 1 means _____.

   a. gentleness

   b. pain or suffering

   c. kindness

3. The word *regulated* in paragraph 2 means _____.

   a. left alone

   b. uncontrolled

   c. governed

4. The word *alleviate* in paragraph 4 means _____.

   a. increase

   b. make worse

   c. relieve

Held Captive

It is the 924th day of my captivity. The humans holding me continue to mock me by speaking in juvenile tones and dangling strange objects before me. It is most displeasing. They further taunt me with their food smells. They sear fine tuna while I am forced to eat cardboard bits.

Today, I attempted to injure the silly humans by kneading them in their sleeping chambers. Tomorrow I shall try weaving around their feet while they move. Each human has only two of them, so this may cause unbalance.

It is the 925th day of my captivity. I slept all day. This evening I decapitated a stuffed mouse and placed it before the vile oppressors who hold me captive. They know not with whom they deal.

It is the 926th day of my captivity. The humans are more ruthless than I even imagined. They subjected me to some form of water torture as I was dipped in vile-smelling chemicals that foamed and bubbled. Then I was exiled to the sleeping chamber.

It is the 927th day of my captivity. The canine is routinely released and then returns, seemingly at will. He must be an accomplice, or else a half-wit. The bird seems to watch my every move. I am certain he is an informant, reporting back to the captors what I do when they leave the dwelling each day.

Answer the questions about the story.

1. Who is the narrator of this story? _____

2. Who are the narrator's captors? _____

3. What was the "water torture"? _____

4. What does the narrator think of the bird and the dog? _____

_____

5. How does the narrator attempt to injure his captors? _____

_____

6. How does the narrator feel about his food? _____

_____

Lewis's World

Clive Staples (C.S.) Lewis, who was known as Jack, was born on November 29, 1898, in Belfast, Ireland, and attended English public schools. During World War I, he served in the British army as an infantry lieutenant and was wounded in battle. Lewis attended Oxford University in England, where he was friends with J.R.R. Tolkien, who later wrote the *Lord of the Rings* books. While at Oxford, Lewis published his first work, *Spirits in Bondage* (1919).

For a large part of his life, C.S. Lewis was an atheist, which is a person who does not believe there is a God. But during the 1920s and 1930s, Lewis underwent a spiritual change. He eventually incorporated his beliefs in Christianity and morality into various works of fiction and nonfiction for children and adults.

The Chronicles of Narnia were published one at a time during the 1950s and were so popular that Lewis received many letters from children who expressed their fascination with the world of Narnia. The books explore the magical world of Narnia, where talking animals and kings, centaurs, and dwarfs exist. They are the best known of Lewis's works, and they are considered children's literary classics. In fact, the final book in the series, *The Last Battle*, even won the British Library Association's Carnegie Medal in 1956.

Answer the questions about the reading.

1. Who wrote *The Chronicles of Narnia*? _____

2. When were the books written? _____

3. Where is the author from? _____

4. What are *The Chronicles of Narnia* about? _____

_____

5. Why did the author write books of a spiritual nature? _____

_____

6. How did the public feel about *The Chronicles of Narnia*? _____

_____

Turkish Delight

Ingredients:

5 tablespoons cornstarch

$\frac{1}{2}$ cup cold water

$\frac{1}{2}$ cup hot water

2 cups sugar

$\frac{1}{2}$ cup orange juice

1 teaspoon lemon juice

2 cups pistachios

1 bag powdered sugar

Directions:

1. Mix cornstarch with cold water and set aside.
2. With an adult's help, bring hot water, sugar, and orange juice to a boil.
3. Add cornstarch and let simmer for 15 minutes, stirring often.
4. Remove from heat and add lemon juice.
5. Stir in nuts.
6. Pour into buttered pan.
7. When cooled and thickened, cut into one-inch cubes with a knife dipped in hot water.
8. Roll in powdered sugar.

Follow the directions.

1. Circle all the ingredients from the list below that are used in Turkish Delight.

| milk | baking soda | eggs | sugar | water |
| flour | cornstarch | chocolate chips | baking powder | orange juice |

2. Underline all the instructions from the list below that are used when making Turkish Delight.

Mix cornstarch with cold water and set aside.

Blend sugar and butter until fluffy.

Add chocolate chips and mix well.

Roll in powdered sugar.

Pour into buttered pan.

Bake at 350 degrees.

Weather Instruments

The term *weather* describes the continuously changing conditions of our environments, including wind, precipitation, and temperature. Those who study weather are called meteorologists. They have many tools to help them understand and predict weather:

Thermometer: measures air temperature

Barometer: measures air pressure

Rain gauge: measures the amount of rain that has fallen over a specific time period

Wind vane: determines the direction from which the wind is blowing

Anemometer: measures wind speed

Hygrometer: measures the water vapor content of air, called humidity

Weather balloon: measures weather conditions higher up in the atmosphere

Compass: a navigational instrument for finding direction

Weather satellite: used to photograph and track large-scale air movements from space

Match each weather instrument to its description.

Barometer	used to photograph and track large-scale air movements from space
Compass	determines the direction from which the wind is blowing
Hygrometer	measures air pressure
Wind vane	measures wind speed
Thermometer	measures the amount of rain that has fallen over a specific time period
Weather satellite	a navigational instrument for finding direction
Anemometer	measures the air temperature
Rain gauge	measures the water vapor content of air

Wildfires

A wildfire is an uncontrolled fire that usually occurs in unpopulated areas. Wildfires can occur anywhere, but they are common in the forested areas of the United States and Canada. The climates in these places allow the growth of trees, but they also have extended dry, hot periods. Wildfires occur particularly in the summer and fall, and during droughts, when fallen branches, leaves, and other material can dry out and become highly flammable. These fires are also common in grasslands and scrublands.

Through arson, which is purposely setting a destructive fire, or just carelessness, a human being starts one out of every four wildfires. Other common causes of wildfires include lightning and volcano eruption. A heat wave, a drought, and a cyclical climate change such as El Niño can increase the odds of a wildfire breakout.

The effects of wildfires can be devastating. When they occur near residential areas, wildfires often destroy homes. For example, in 2007, extensive wildfires burning in southern California destroyed about 500,000 acres of land and forced nearly 900,000 people to evacuate their homes. In addition, the secondary effects of wildfires—erosion, landslides, introduction of invasive species, and changes in water quality—are often more disastrous than the fire itself.

Write *true* or *false* after each statement about the reading.

1. A cause of a wildfire is lightning. _____

2. An effect of a wildfire is change in water quality. _____

3. A cause of a wildfire is evacuation of homes. _____

4. An effect of a wildfire is arson. _____

5. A cause of a wildfire is human carelessness. _____

6. An effect of a wildfire is erosion. _____

Today's Weather

As you read the forecast, fill in each blank with any word from the correct part of speech. Have fun!

The weather will turn _____ over the Northeast on Sunday. A
ADJECTIVE

potent windy _____ and much colder air will
NOUN

_____. West to northwest _____ across
VERB   PLURAL NOUN

the Mid-Atlantic, upstate _____, and New England could gust
PLACE

to _____ mph at times. Daytime _____
NUMBER   PLURAL NOUN

on Sunday will be in the 30s from _____ to
COUNTRY

_____. Wind chills will be _____ low,
PLACE   ADVERB

_____ in northwest Pennsylvania and western New York, while
VERB ENDING IN "ING"

_____ snows will _____ fall from the
ADJECTIVE   ADVERB

_____ of West Virginia.
PLURAL NOUN

Weather in My Life

Have you ever experienced an intense weather phenomenon, such as a blizzard, hurricane, or tornado? Write a story explaining a personal weather experience.

_____

_____

_____

_____

_____

_____

_____

_____

_____

_____

_____

_____

_____

_____

Acid Rain

Rain is very important for life. All living things need water to live. But in many places in the world, rain has become a menace. Pollution in the air and acid gases from factories, cars, and homes are just a few of the things that can make rain unhealthy. This poison rain is known as acid rain.

The negative effects of acid rain are numerous. Acid rain accelerates the decay of buildings. The acid eats into metal and stone and damages stained glass and plastics. In many places in the world, famous historical buildings and monuments are affected by acid rain. For example, the Statue of Liberty had to be restored because of acid rain damage.

Acid rain is damaging to the health of human beings, too. Water we drink from taps can be contaminated by acid rain, which can damage the brain. Acid rain also has frightful effects on forests. The acid removes important minerals from the leaves and the soil. Without them, trees and plants cannot grow properly. They lose their leaves and become weak. This makes them more vulnerable to illnesses and frost.

The ecological effects of acid rain are most clear in aquatic environments, such as streams, lakes, and marshes. Even if the acid rain does not fall directly into a body of water, it can enter from rivers and streams. Fish and plants cannot survive in acidic lakes, so the lake eventually "dies." For example, there are thousands of "dead" lakes in Scandinavia that received so much acid rain that the lake ecosystem died out.

Answer the questions about the reading.

1. What are two causes of acid rain? _____

_____

2. What are two effects of acid rain? _____

_____

3. Which of the following steps could help keep the air clean and prevent acid rain? Underline them.

People could use buses or trains instead of cars.

People could drive their cars more.

People could buy hybrid cars.

People could keep buying cars that make the air dirty.

Greenhouse Effect

The phenomenon known as the *greenhouse effect* is the rise in temperature that the earth experiences as a result of gases in the atmosphere trapping energy from the sun, like in a greenhouse. These gases prevent heat, in the form of infrared radiation, from escaping back into space, making earth's average temperature appropriate for life. Without these gases, earth would be about 60°F colder.

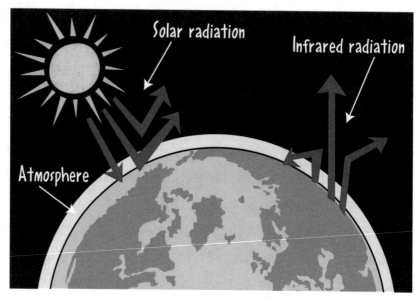

The danger of the greenhouse effect would come if it were to get stronger. If earth became warmer than usual, humans, plants, and animals would all face life-threatening problems.

Use the reading and diagram to answer the questions.

1. Through what does solar radiation pass to get to earth? _____

2. What happens to most of it? _____

_____

3. What happens to the rest of it? _____

_____

4. What is later emitted from the surface of earth? _____

5. Where does it go? _____

_____

_____

6. What is the effect of this? _____

D'oh!

Matt Groening is a cartoonist who was born in Portland, Oregon, in 1954. He studied at The Evergreen State College in Olympia, Washington, and then moved to Los Angeles, California, in 1977. He was intent on becoming a writer.

Groening joined the staff of the *Los Angeles Reader* and began contributing a comic strip in order to vent his frustrations about living in Los Angeles. The strip was about two rabbits that were constantly bummed out.

A producer at Fox Broadcasting Company enjoyed Groening's work, so he asked Groening to create something for television. Groening came up with the idea for *The Simpsons*, a cartoon family featuring dad Homer, mother Marge, and children Bart, Lisa, and Maggie. In 1987, a one-minute long *The Simpsons* aired during a popular Fox show. Needless to say, it was a massive hit.

The brief cartoon featuring everyone's favorite family was so popular that it became its own series. *The Simpsons* debuted on December 17, 1989. The show has experienced immense success: It won an Emmy for Best Animated Series in 1990, and in 2007, *The Simpsons* celebrated its record-setting 400th episode. Matt Groening has won 10 Emmy awards, nine for *The Simpsons* and one for another animated series he launched in 1999.

The Simpsons has become a billion-dollar empire, including books and toys related to *The Simpsons*. There was even a major motion picture about the Simpsons, which hit the big screen in 2007.

Unscramble the words mentioned in the reading.

1. hte pssimons _____

2. oocartn _____

3. attm grongeni _____

4. memy _____

5. brta _____

6. omher _____

Michelangelo's Masterpiece

The Sistine Chapel is the chapel in the Apostolic Palace, which is the official residence of the Pope. Located in the Vatican City in Rome, Italy, it is famous for its architecture, its purpose—the place where a new Pope is chosen and other activities by the Pope—and its famous decoration. The Sistine Chapel was built between 1475 and 1483 and named after Sixtus IV, the Pope who had it built. In 1508, Pope Julius II requested that the ceiling of the Sistine Chapel be repainted, and he commissioned none other than the renowned artist Michelangelo to do the job.

The ceiling of the Sistine Chapel was originally painted like a blue sky with gold stars. Instead Pope Julius II wanted to see paintings of the twelve Apostles created on the ceiling, but he got much more than that.

Michelangelo spent most of the next four years painting what has become one of the world's most beloved pieces of artwork. Michelangelo discarded the Pope's original design idea and created something entirely different. He produced paintings that illustrate nine stories from the Bible's Book of Genesis, which included more than 3,000 figures. The realistic depictions of some of Judaism's and Christianity's most famous moments are a spectacular artistic display. He also did the entire thing himself. Typically, artists commissioned to do such large-scale pieces would have brought in additional artists to help them, but not Michelangelo.

Painting the Sistine Chapel's ceiling was not without obstacle. The ceiling is nearly 68 feet off the ground, so how could Michelangelo paint on it—for four years? He would have to lie on his back, which required scaffolding to raise him close enough to the ceiling to do so. The artist built his own scaffold, which was held in place by brackets connected

to the walls. Another potential obstacle for Michelangelo was mold. Mold could have been disastrous for the work, because it had the potential to make the plaster wet and crumbly. So Michelangelo's assistant developed plaster that would stay dry, thereby eliminating the problem.

Michelangelo also had to endure the critical eye of the Pope, who wanted to repeatedly see the ceiling up close as it was being created. Unfortunately, another of Michelangelo's obstacles was a financial one. The Pope was slow to pay the artist for his work, so Michelangelo struggled for four long years to complete it, during which time he had to support his family.

Despite all of these hurdles, Michelangelo completed the ceiling of the Sistine Chapel. On November 1, 1512, the masterpiece was revealed to the world. Pope Julius II was very pleased with the result, as were all who would view it afterward.

The creation of the Sistine Chapel's ceiling did take its toll on Michelangelo, though. For a year after its completion, the artist needed other people to read for him. Four years of intense detail work had temporarily marred his vision.

Answer the questions about the reading.

1. Who painted the Sistine Chapel and why? _____

_____

2. What is the Sistine Chapel? _____

_____

3. What were two of the artist's obstacles in painting the Sistine Chapel? _____

_____

_____

4. What was one effect of his having painted the Sistine Chapel? _____

_____

5. How do you think the artist felt about being commissioned to paint the Sistine Chapel?

_____

6. How would you describe the artist in a word? _____

7. What things in the story lead you to think that about the artist? _____

_____

_____

Flower Child

Georgia O'Keeffe is widely considered one of the greatest American artists of the 20th century. She was born on November 15, 1887, in Sun Prairie, Wisconsin and began making art at a young age. O'Keeffe studied at the Art Institute of Chicago in the early 1900s. Later, she lived in New York City and studied with such artists as William Merritt Chase as a member of the Art Students League.

In 1916, a friend of O'Keeffe's showed her work to a famous photographer named Alfred Stieglitz. He was the owner of a well-known art gallery in New York where he displayed O'Keeffe's artwork to the public. O'Keeffe and Stieglitz formed a professional and personal partnership. They married in 1924.

Some of O'Keeffe's popular works came from this early period of her career. They include pieces such as *Black Iris* (1926) and *Oriental Poppies* (1928). Her first paintings were abstractions of light and shape. Over time, it evolved to become more recognizable things, but viewed from unusual angles.

In the late 1920s, Georgia O'Keeffe fell in love with the Southwest. She spent every summer there for 17 years and when her husband died in 1946, she moved there for good. She used the Southwest's rugged setting as further inspiration for her artwork.

Georgia O'Keeffe died on March 6, 1986, in Santa Fe, New Mexico. Her artwork can be viewed at museums worldwide and the Georgia O'Keeffe Museum in Santa Fe.

Answer the questions about the reading. Circle the letter of the answer.

1. The author's purpose is _____.

    a. to inform

    b. to entertain

    c. to persuade

2. As a child, Georgia O'Keeffe could have been described as _____.

    a. dull

    b. uncreative

    c. precocious

3. Georgia O'Keeffe used her surroundings as sources of _____.

    a. criticism

    b. inspiration

    c. remorse

4. Georgia O'Keeffe's early works can be described as _____.

    a. realistic

    b. bland

    c. abstract

Splatter Man

Jackson Pollock was an American painter who pioneered a new style, called Abstract Expressionism. His work raised the eyebrows of more traditional critics, but Pollock has become known as one of the twentieth century's finest artists.

Jackson Pollock was born in 1912 in Cody, Wyoming, but was raised in Arizona and California. In 1930, Pollock moved to New York City to join his brother. That is where he met his future wife, Lee Krasner, who would later influence his work.

Pollock's style was unusual, sometimes referred to as "Action Painting." Pollock would lay large canvases on the floor and then move around above them, dripping, pouring, and splattering paint. Critics nicknamed him "Jack the Dripper." Sometimes he would use a brush, but other times, he would just pour the paint or use his hands and other objects to create texture. He utilized things like sand, bottle caps, nails, and even cigarettes.

Pollock's work drew the attention of Peggy Guggenheim, the wealthy New York heiress whose family is responsible for the famed Guggenheim Museum. She commissioned Pollock to create his first large-scale piece of art, entitled *Mural* (1943), and became his dealer and patron.

Pollock and Lee Krasner eventually moved to Long Island, where Pollock began creating more large-scale artwork. These enormous pieces would become his hallmark. Pollock's work was both praised and dismissed. Some critics simply brushed him off as eccentric, but others recognized the genius of his work.

Pollock had become widely known in the New York art scene, but his work was introduced to the masses in 1949, when *Life* magazine published an article about him. Sadly, Pollock was killed in a car accident in 1956, but he remains an artistic visionary.

Write *fact* or *opinion* after each statement from the reading.

1. Large-scale, colorful pieces were Jackson Pollock's hallmark. _____

2. Some referred to his style as Action Painting. _____

3. Pollock remains an artistic visionary. _____

4. Jackson Pollock was an American painter. _____

5. Pollock was eccentric and not a real artist. _____

You Be the Artist

Imagine that someone famous and important chose you to create a painting. What would it look like? Where would you make it? Use the drawing space to create your own masterpiece, and use the lines to explain it.

_____

_____

_____

_____

_____

Or, if you'd like to mimic the work of Jackson Pollock (neatly) and you have access to a computer, you can go to: www.jacksonpollock.org. Click on the screen to begin your virtual painting. Move the mouse around and click to create drips and splatters in different colors.

Garden of Love

If you wanted to create a special garden for someone you love, for whom would it be? Where would you build your garden, and what would you include in it? Write about your garden on the lines below. Then, draw a picture of your garden in the space provided.

_____

_____

_____

_____

_____

_____

Write On

This chart lists the types of **nonfiction** writing and their characteristics.

TYPE OF NONFICTION	TRAITS	AUTHOR'S PURPOSE
Autobiography or Biography	written about a person's life or one main event; has a plot; can be read in one sitting or have many chapters	to inform
Encyclopedia	information organized by topic; topics organized alphabetically; entries are short; used for research	to inform
Essay	can be read in one sitting; can be based on research or personal experience; written in paragraph form, usually five or more paragraphs	to persuade; to entertain; to inform
Feature Story	focuses on one topic or main idea; has a plot	to entertain; to inform
Interview	can be read in one sitting to entertain; recorded word for word; may be written in bullet format or like a drama	to entertain; to inform
Newspaper Article	short; can be read in one sitting; focuses on one topic or main idea	to persuade; to inform
Textbook	used for reference; information organized by topic; organized chronologically (in time sequence) or by topic	to inform

This chart lists the types of **fiction** writing and their characteristics.

TYPE OF FICTION	TRAITS	COMPONENTS
Short Story	can be easily read in one sitting; explores one topic	*Plot*: events of the story *Characters*: people, animals, or imaginary characters in the story
Novel	has a longer, more complicated plot	*Setting*: time and place in which the story occurs *Theme*: main message of the story

Write *F* or *N* next to each statement to tell if it describes fiction or nonfiction.

1. _____ A short story is an example.

2. _____ A biography is written to inform.

3. _____ Characteristics of it are plot, characters, setting, and theme.

4. _____ An essay is an example.

5. _____ A newspaper article is an example.

6. _____ Novels generally have a long, complicated plot.

7. _____ An interview can be published in order to entertain.

8. _____ An encyclopedia article is an example.

Unsightly Offspring

There once was a duck family that lived on a farm. Mother Duck had been sitting on a clutch of new eggs, and soon out popped six perfectly lovely, chirpy ducklings. The seventh duckling, however, had gray feathers rather than soft, yellow, downy ones. "Poor little ugly duckling!" Mother Duck would say. "Why are you so different from the others?" She couldn't imagine why one of her children looked so vastly different.

The ugly duckling was gloomy. His mother felt that he was unsightly, and his siblings would not play with him. He secretly wept at night. Nobody liked an ugly duckling. Feeling entirely unwanted, one morning at sunrise the ugly duckling ran away from home. He stopped at a pond and questioned the other birds, "Do you know of any ducklings with gray feathers like mine?" The other birds shook their heads in distaste and replied, "We don't know any birds as ugly as you."

The ugly duckling continued to another pond, but there a pair of large geese gave him the same answer to his question. They also warned him that hunters were on the prowl. Cheerless and frightened, the duckling wished he had never left the farmyard.

One day, the ugly duckling's travels took him by a cottage in the country. The old woman who inhabited the cottage thought that he was a stray goose, so she captured the ugly duckling. She hoped that he would lay plenty of eggs, but alas, the duckling did not lay a single egg. The other animals at the cottage teased the duckling, "Just wait! If you don't lay eggs, the old woman will wring your neck and pop you into the pot!" The ugly duckling was thoroughly terrified, and so one night, he escaped the cottage. He sought to be loved, not to be cooked!

All alone in the world again, the ugly duckling found solace in a bed of reeds. "I'll hide here forever," he said. And though he was lonely, at least he was safe and free from scorn. One day at sunrise, the ugly duckling spied a flock of beautiful birds soaring overhead. He longed to resemble the lovely birds, even just for a day.

But then winter crept in and the reed bed froze. The ugly duckling found himself  cold and hungry, and so he moved on to find food and shelter once again. Weary from hunger and worry, the ugly duckling dropped to the ground, exhausted. That is where a farmer found him.

The farmer took pity on the poor, almost frozen duckling and brought him to his house, where the duckling was showered with care. The ugly duckling stayed with the farmer and his family through the bitter winter. By spring, the duckling had grown quite large and the farmer thought it best to set the creature free by the pond.

The ugly duckling walked toward the pond's edge and caught his reflection in its surface. That was when the duckling saw himself mirrored in the water. "Goodness! How I've changed! I hardly recognize myself!" he said. Just then, the flock of beautiful birds he'd seen many months before flew overhead again.

The flock swept down to see the creature that they recognized as one of their own. "Where have you been hiding?" they questioned. "We have been seeking you." That was when the duckling realized that he was not, in fact, an ugly duckling. He was a swan, and a beautiful one, too. He dashed into the pond, where he and his fellow swans majestically swam together.

On the side of the pond, he even heard one of the kind farmer's children proclaim, "Look at that young swan! He's the finest of them all!" And the former ugly duckling blushed. He was happy. He recalled how he had been despised, and he rejoiced, "I never dreamed of so much happiness when I was the ugly duckling!"

Answer the questions about the story.

1. At the beginning of the story, how is the ugly duckling made to feel? _____

_____

2. Do you feel that he should have been treated the way he was? _____

3. Why do you think he was treated this way? _____

_____

4. Who rescues the ugly duckling? _____

5. How is he treated from that time forward? _____

_____

6. How does the ugly duckling feel by the end of the story? _____

_____

The Goose and the Golden Eggs

There once was a countryman who lived a simple, humble life. One day, the countryman went to the nest of the goose he kept. When he moved to retrieve the goose's egg, he found a very special egg awaiting him. The egg was glittering yellow in color and felt quite heavy, like lead.

The countryman thought for certain that a prankster was playing a trick on him, for no goose's egg was heavy like lead or sparkled like gold. Nevertheless, the countryman took the egg home with him. That was when the countryman realized that the reason the goose egg was heavy and yellow was because it was made of solid gold.

Every morning from that day forward, the goose produced another golden egg. The countryman was astounded, but excited, for he knew that gold eggs would be quite valuable. The countryman began selling his golden eggs, and, as he predicted, he quickly grew wealthy. This change was welcome to the countryman, who was tired of feeling distressed by poverty. But as the countryman grew rich, he also grew greedy. He concocted the idea that the goose must be laden with golden eggs, and he wanted those eggs more than one at a time. He wanted them all immediately!

So the countryman slaughtered his special goose to open it up and retrieve its golden eggs. But the countryman found nothing of the sort inside, and, sadly, now his magical goose was dead.

Answer the questions about the story.

1. What did the countryman first think about the glittering egg? _____

_____

2. What was really so special about the goose egg? _____

3. Why was the countryman excited about this? _____

4. What was the result of all of this? _____

_____

5. What do you think the moral of this story is? _____

_____

Cells

Cells are the building blocks of life. All living things are composed of them. Cells are small compartments that hold all of the biological equipment necessary to keep an organism alive.

Some living things are unicellular, which means they consist of just one cell (*uni-* means "one"). Microscopic organisms, such as bacteria and protozoa, are examples of unicellular forms of life. Other living things are multicellular, meaning they are composed of many cells working together. Plants, animals, and fungi are examples of multicellular organisms.

Cells come in an enormous range of sizes. The smallest cell can measure just 0.000004 inch in diameter and are found in organisms called mycoplasmas. If you lined up 10,000 mycoplasmas in a row, they would only be as wide as the diameter of a human hair!

Some of the largest cells in existence can be found in animals, such as the giraffe. The nerve cells that run down a giraffe's neck can exceed 9.7 feet in length—just one cell! Human cells come in a variety of sizes, and include anything from small, red blood cells that measure 0.00003 inch to liver cells, which may be ten times larger. About 10,000 typical human cells could fit on the head of a pin.

Regardless of how many or what size they are, cells are marvels of design and efficiency. Cells carry out thousands of biochemical reactions each minute and reproduce new cells, which perpetuate life.

Find six terms from the reading in the word puzzle below.

U	N	I	C	E	L	L	U	L	A	R	F	O
T	S	C	U	E	E	F	W	N	C	X	G	R
E	R	B	I	O	L	O	G	Y	E	O	N	G
R	O	N	D	S	N	R	O	C	P	U	F	A
N	D	N	E	E	O	M	S	V	T	E	K	N
E	S	C	W	O	G	A	T	O	O	E	I	I
T	E	E	O	U	W	T	U	L	R	G	N	S
R	I	L	I	F	E	O	D	U	S	K	F	M
D	Y	L	D	W	O	I	J	M	M	N	U	X
M	U	L	T	I	C	E	L	L	U	L	A	R

Plant Cells

Cell membrane: thin layer of protein and fat that surrounds the cell, but is inside the cell wall

Cell wall: thick, rigid membrane that surrounds a plant cell

Centrosome: small body located near the nucleus; it has a dense center and radiating tubules

Chloroplast: elongated or disc-shaped organelle containing chlorophyll

Cristae: folded inner membrane of a plant cell's mitochondrion; finger-like projections

Cytoplasm: jelly-like material outside the cell nucleus in which the organelles are located

Golgi body: flattened, layered, sac-like organelle; resembles a stack of pancakes and located near the nucleus

Mitochondrion: spherical or rod-shaped organelle with a double membrane; the inner membrane is infolded many times, forming a series of projections called cristae

Nucleus: spherical body containing many organelles, including the nucleolus; the nucleus is surrounded by the nuclear membrane

Nuclear membrane: membrane that surrounds the nucleus

Nucleolus: organelle within the nucleus

Ribosome: small organelle composed of cytoplasmic granules

Rough endoplasmic reticulum: vast system of interconnected, membranous, infolded, and convoluted sacs that are located in the cell's cytoplasm; covered with ribosomes

Smooth endoplasmic reticulum: vast system of interconnected, membranous, infolded, and convoluted tubes; located in the cytoplasm

Vacuole: large, membrane-bound space; filled with fluid; a single vacuole often takes up much of the cell

Use your knowledge of cell structure and the descriptions to label the parts of a plant cell.

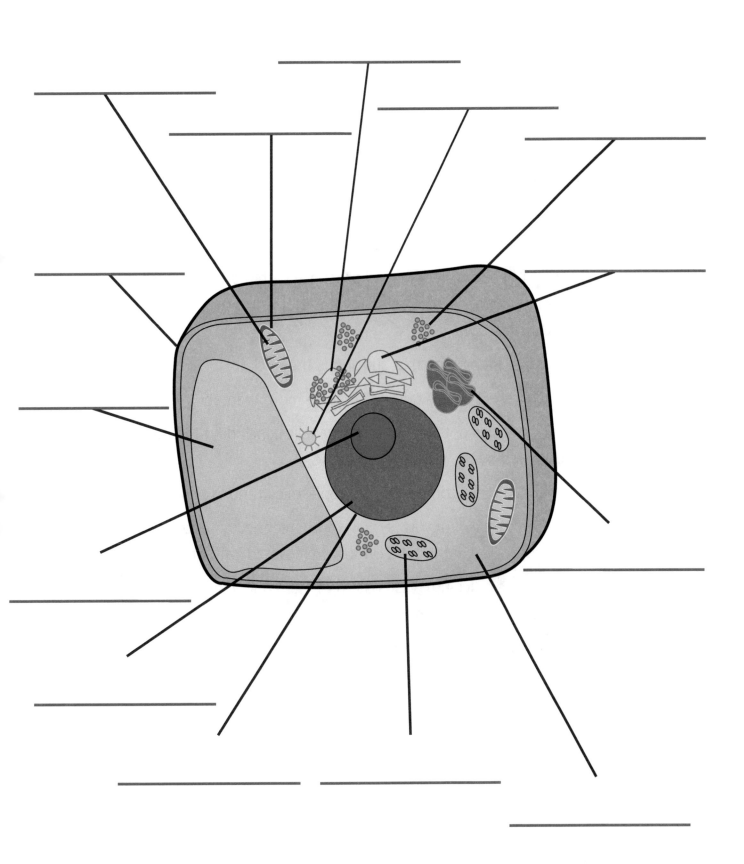

Animal Cells

Cell membrane: thin layer of protein and fat that surrounds the cell

Centrosome: small body located near the nucleus; has a dense center and radiating tubules

Cytoplasm: jelly-like material outside the cell nucleus in which the organelles are located

Golgi body: flattened, layered, sac-like organelle; resembles a stack of pancakes; located near the nucleus

Lysosome: round organelle surrounded by a membrane

Mitochondrion: spherical or rod-shaped organelle with a double membrane; inner membrane is infolded many times, forming a series of projections called cristae

Nuclear membrane: membrane that surrounds the nucleus

Nucleolus: organelle within the nucleus; may be more than one present

Nucleus: spherical body containing many organelles, including the nucleolus; surrounded by the nuclear membrane

Ribosome: small organelle composed of cytoplasmic granules

Rough endoplasmic reticulum: vast system of interconnected and convoluted sacs that are located in the cell's cytoplasm; covered with ribosomes

Smooth endoplasmic reticulum: vast system of interconnected, convoluted tubes; located in the cytoplasm

Vacuole: fluid-filled, membrane-surrounded cavity inside a cell

Use your knowledge of cell structure and the descriptions to label the parts of an animal cell.

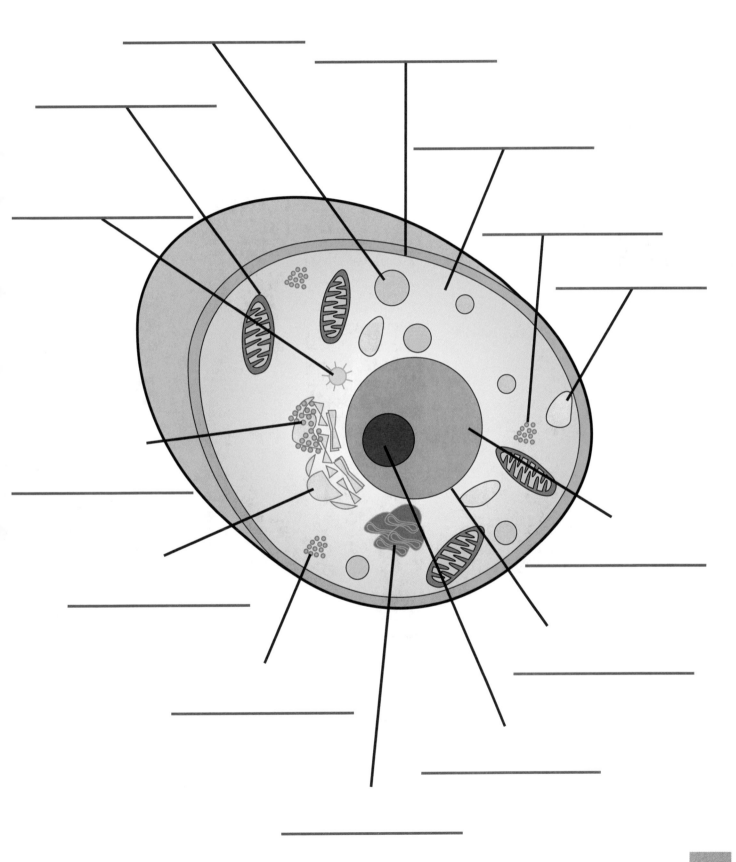

Answer Key

Page 6
1. true
2. false
3. true
4. true
5. false
6. true

Page 7

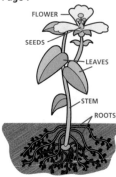

FLOWER
SEEDS
LEAVES
STEM
ROOTS

Page 8
1. the process by which seeds grow into new plants
2. stamens
3. pollen
4. ovule
5. Pollen must move from a stamen to the stigma.
6. Insects accidentally rub pollen onto the stigma.

Page 9
1. tomatoes
2. seeds
3. vegetable
4. botanists
5. ovary
6. roots

Page 10
1. The following should be underlined: 2 Tbsp.
2. The following should be underlined: 1 cup
3. The following should be underlined: 4–5
4. Have an adult help you purée until smooth.
5. possible answers: The smoothie will be thicker, creamier, and heavier. The smoothie will have more fat and calories.
6. Answers will vary.

Page 11
1. b
2. c
3. a
4. a

Page 12
1. trees
2. trunk
3. stands
4. Forests
5. General Sherman Tree
6. South America

Page 13
3 Morton quickly planted many trees and other plants near his new home.
1 Morton moved from Detroit, Michigan, to what was the Nebraska Territory.
4 Morton became a prominent figure in the local area.
6 Arbor Day was made a legal holiday in Nebraska.
2 Morton found that Nebraska was generally a treeless place.
5 Morton attended a meeting of the State Board of Agriculture, where he suggested a tree-planting holiday.

Pages 14–15

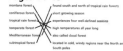

montane forest — found south and north of tropical rain forests
coniferous forest — short growing season
tropical rain forest — experiences four well-defined seasons
temperate forest — high temperatures all year long
Mediterranean forest — also called cloud forest
subtropical forest — located in cold, windy regions near the North and South poles

Page 16
1. fact
2. opinion
3. fact
4. fact
5. fact
6. opinion

Page 17
1. Cassius Marcellus Clay
2. 1942
3. twelve years old
4. Parkinson's disease
5. "Float like a butterfly, sting like a bee"
6. three

Page 18

1974 — Henry (Hank) Aaron was born.
1982 — Hank Aaron was awarded the Presidential Medal of Freedom.
2002 — Barry Bonds broke Hank Aaron's career home-run record.
2007 — Hank Aaron started playing for the Major League.
1982 — Hank Aaron was elected to the National Baseball Hall of Fame.
1974 — Hank Aaron hit his 715th home run.

Page 19
Stories will vary.

Page 20
1. Bela Karolyi
2. 1984
3. possible answers: She won a gold medal in the women's all-around, making her the first female gymnast to do this who was not from Eastern Europe; she scored a perfect 10.
4. 1986
5. She was granted membership in the International Gymnastics Hall of Fame.

Page 21
1. a
2. b
3. c
4. c

Page 22
1. at a very young age
2. 1996
3. 2006
4. 1997
5. 2001

Page 23
1. skates
2. speed skating
3. world record
4. Olympics
5. gold
6. glide

Page 24
1. on a soccer field
2. Sam
3. possible answers: nervous, excited, anxious, psyched up
4. Sam has long, muscular legs, short, brown hair, and she is wearing a green-and-white jersey and shorts.
5. Jessica is small and stocky and has blond hair.

Page 25

Page 26
1. Wimbledon
2. 19
3. female athlete
4. International Tennis Hall of Fame
5. Long Beach, California
6. Bobby Riggs

Page 27
Stories will vary.

Page 28
1. skyhook
2. UCLA
3. Milwaukee Bucks
4. 38,387
5. 6

Page 29

C F O X H O U N D F B C V
R V A Q E I O A O U D O Q
J A M E S T O W N F T M A
R S Z O I E N I B E Z M O
S U V D V D V O C V U O Q
T A N Q E O C S I U W D R
E C C A O G A T S F E W E
B E F O U F U E L D I N N
R I C H M O N D I S T A N
D Y Q B W O V J Q M I L K
D C G Z A D Z O U T Z T A
B E R W A E V O E S N H V

Pages 30–31
1. near Charlottesville, Virginia, in central Virginia, on a mountain
2. 25
3. little mountain
4. 40 years
5. 56 years
6. 11,000 square feet
7. The building materials and additional water had to be transported uphill.
8. France

Pages 32–33
1. William Henry Harrison
2. 8
3. He was the first president to make a radio broadcast.
4. Barboursville, Virginia
5. William Henry Harrison
6. Mount Vernon, Virginia
7. Thomas Jefferson
8. John Tyler

Page 34
1. false
2. false
3. true
4. false
5. true

Page 35
1. a group of Native American Algonquian tribes
2. the area that is now the state of Virginia
3. Powhatan; Wahunsenacah or Wahunsenacawh
4. The British were taking over lands that belonged to Powhatan and his people.
5. Powhatan's daughter
6. his brother Opechancanough

Page 36
1. Powhatan
2. Matoaka
3. John Smith
4. John Rolfe
5. Jamestown

Page 37
Stories will vary, but should be different from the traditional ending, in which the moral is that appearances can be deceiving.

Page 38
1. b
2. a
3. a
4. b

Page 39
1. Studies show that we sleep better in a cool place.
2. It can keep you awake at night.
3. the same time you wake up during the week
4. If all you do in bed is sleep, your brain learns that bed equals sleep, which will help you fall asleep much faster.

Page 40
1. R
2. I
3. I
4. R
5. R

Page 41
1. 90 minutes
2. 5
3. REM; Rapid Eye Movement
4. dreaming
5. groggy and confused
6. being awake and very relaxed

Page 42
1. dream
2. paralysis
3. rapid eye movement
4. sleepwalking
5. Sigmund Freud
6. brain

Page 43
Answers will vary.

Page 44
1. ultraviolet
2. Sun Protection Factor
3. a lot; it should be applied liberally or generously
4. every few hours
5. not see-through

Page 45
Stories will vary, but should relate to a shark or dolphin in the water, or other things illustrated in the scene.

Page 46
1. Diabetes is a disease in which there is too much sugar in the blood.
2. The body either has trouble producing enough insulin or is unable to use the insulin it does produce.
3. possible answers: higher risk of heart attack, stroke, blindness, kidney failure, blood circulation problems.
4. Type 1 happens when the immune system attacks the cells that make insulin. Without the insulin, diabetes develops. Unlike type 1, those with type-2 diabetes have bodies that do produce insulin. But the body either doesn't make enough insulin or it is just unable to use the insulin it has.

Page 47

<u>2</u> Food enters the esophagus.

<u>5</u> Then food actually moves upward in the ascending colon.

<u>1</u> The process of chewing begins to break down the food.

<u>6</u> Waste product is stored in the rectum until you go to the bathroom, when it leaves the body through the anus.

<u>3</u> Then food heads to the jejunum.

<u>4</u> Inside the stomach, food mixes with gastric acid.

Page 48
1. microbe
2. everywhere
3. They make you sick.
4. Wash your hands.
5. possible answers: before preparing food, before eating, before touching wounds, after using the restroom, after blowing your nose, after playing with a dog

Page 49
1. true
2. false
3. true
4. true
5. true
6. false

Page 50
1. Edmund Hillary and Tenzing Norgay
2. It sits on the border of Nepal and Tibet in Asia.
3. 29,035 feet
4. the Himalayas
5. -76° F
6. high winds, snow, height

Page 51
1. fish
2. great barrier reef
3. coral reef
4. limestone
5. Australia
6. skeletons

Page 52
Drawings will vary, but image should depict a coral reef with sea life surrounding it, such as fish and sharks.

Page 53
1. Arizona
2. 6,000 feet at its deepest point
3. The Colorado River carved through rock layers.
4. more than 2 billion years old
5. It can be found in only a specific place.
6. four million

Page 54
1. c
2. b
3. b
4. c
5. a
6. a

Page 55
1. Brazil
2. The Atlantic Ocean eroded the soil and rocks along the coast.
3. and 4. Sugarloaf Mountain; Corcovado Peak; Christ the Redeemer
5. Guanabara Bay
6. River of January

Page 56
1. 1943
2. possible answers: Paricutin is the first volcano to have known witnesses at its birth; it is the fastest-growing volcano in history; Paricutin is the most recent volcano to have formed on the Western Hemisphere; it is considered one of the Seven Wonders of the Natural World.
3. Mexico
4. possible answers: It buried most of the town of Paricutin and partially buried its neighbor, San Juan Parangricutiro; they lost crops, livestock, and suffered substantial damage to their property.
5. 1952
6. none

Page 57
Drawings will vary, but should depict a volcano exploding from the ground.

Page 58

Page 59
1. 7
2. Great Barrier Reef
3. 3
4. Victoria Falls
5. 7
6. the Harbor at Rio de Janeiro

Pages 60–61
1. Khufu
2. skilled laborers
3. compass
4. ramps
5. bedrock
6. clay
7. acres
8. Nile River

Pages 62–63

Pages 64–65
1. Nebudchadnezzar II
2. The king wanted to make his wife, Amyitis, happier and more comfortable by building her a series of gorgeous gardens that would remind her of her homeland.
3. No, the gardens were actually built on a mountainside, and draped down.
4. The gardens were in the ancient metropolis of Babylon, which sat about 50 miles south of modern-day Baghdad, Iraq. This area was in the Mesopotamian desert.
5. The gardens were essentially impossible to create because of the desert climate.
6. possible answers: There are no historical records of it, other than stories; Excavations at Babylon have not found any trace of this desert oasis; Another story circulating among scholars is that the gardens were built not by Nebudchadnezzar II, but rather by the Assyrian queen Semiramis.

Page 66
1. a
2. c
3. a
4. b

Page 67
1. Greece
2. more than 800 years
3. the architect Libon
4. Phidias, a renowned Greek sculptor
5. about 43 feet
6. a statue of Nike, the goddess of victory

Page 68
1. false
2. false
3. true
4. true
5. false
6. true

Page 69
1. The Pharos lit the way for sailors navigating the harbor into Alexandria.
2. A fire at the top guided ships during the night. During the day, polished bronze mirrors reflected sunlight out to sea.
3. on the ancient island of Pharos, which was just off the coast of the Egyptian city of Alexandria
4. Several earthquakes destroyed most of the famed lighthouse.
5. Construction began around 300 BCE.
6. The total height was about 400 feet, making the Pharos of Alexandria the tallest manmade structure on earth for many centuries.

Page 70
1. Artemisia
2. Greek
3. tomb
4. mausoleum
5. Halicarnassus
6. Turkey

Page 71
Answers will vary.

Page 72
Answers will vary, but should reflect indicated parts of speech.

Page 73
1. Mayan
2. The sun moves through the zenith passage.
3. Light and shadow create the appearance of a snake slithering down the stairway of the pyramid.
4. The Mayan people likely used El Castillo to track the seasons, which would have let them know when to plant, harvest, and perform ceremonies.

Page 74

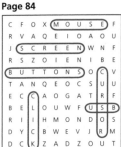

Page 75
1. It was an ellipse, which prevented the players from retreating to a corner while allowing spectators to be closer to the action.
2. a cooling system
3. Roman aristocrats
4. gladiators
5. The Roman Colosseum was damaged by fire in 217 CE. Then it was the victim of several earthquakes between 442 and 1349 that continued to destroy the structure.

Page 76
1. fact
2. opinion
3. fact
4. opinion
5. fact
6. fact

Page 77
1. 3,106 miles
2. as a form of protection from possible enemies
3. The process of building it was so tremendous and time consuming that it was impossible to build it with uniform forms and materials.
4. Qin Shi Huangdi
5. Ming Dynasty

Page 78
1. c
2. a
3. b
4. a

Page 79
1. Incan
2. Peru
3. It stands on a ridge between two peaks about 1,950 feet above the Urubamba River below.
4. 1911
5. 15th century
6. a smallpox outbreak

Pages 80–81
1. became or acted as a friend to
2. discontented or angry
3. to place too low a value on
4. to feel intense hatred toward
5. dirtying, staining, or infecting by contact or association
6. wetted with liquid
7. rejecting lawful or conventional behavior
8. to deal with successfully

Page 82

<u>3</u> Stir until butter coats macaroni.

<u>5</u> Bake, uncovered, at 325 degrees for 1½ hours until golden brown and creamy.

<u>1</u> Melt butter in a baking dish.

<u>4</u> Add salt, pepper, cheese, and milk to macaroni.

<u>2</u> Pour macaroni into melted butter.

Answers may vary, but the macaroni and cheese would not taste right.

Page 83
1. possible answers: any environment all over the world; fields; human habitats
2. anything from seeds and grass to fruit and bugs
3. 3 to 14 inches
4. Their front teeth grow throughout their life and must be worn down.
5. possible answers: cats, dogs, owls, hawks, humans
6. between $\frac{1}{4}$ and 2 ounces

Page 84

Page 85
1. He loved his life and home. He felt satisfied.
2. He makes the country mouse feel badly about the way in which he lives his life, as though life in the city is much better.
3. He does not like the city. There is a scary cat at the house!
4. possible answers: To each his own; everyone has different preferences, and they are all acceptable.

Page 86
1. 1928
2. Walt Disney
3. possible answers: He is a "good guy"; he has a sunny outlook on life; his personality is boyish and enthusiastic; he always shows positive values; he represents the ideal person that many people would like to be; he is humble.
4. Drawings will vary.

Page 87
1. false
2. false
3. true
4. false
5. true
6. true

Pages 88–89

Pages 90–91

Page 92
1. Writing an e-mail message with the caps-lock function is like screaming over e-mail.
2. The Internet is not a safe or private place.
3. No, emoticons should be avoided.
4. No, always make an e-mail message shorter than you would a letter.
5. E-mails with bad grammar or no punctuation are difficult to read and can sometimes even change the meaning of the message.

Page 93

Page 94
Letters will vary, but should reflect the situation and use the appropriate tone, such as:

Dear Aunt Sally,

I absolutely love the sweater you sent me for Christmas—thanks! Blue is my favorite color, and the cashmere feels so luxurious against my skin.

Best wishes,
Bailey

Page 95
1. Preheat the oven.
2. The cookies will not cook quickly enough.
3. More salt is added later.
4. The cookies would burn.

Page 96
1. c
2. b
3. a
4. b

Page 97
1. false
2. true
3. true
4. false
5. true
6. true

Pages 98–99
1. entertain
2. fantasy
3. Christopher becomes a cookie, and other people eat Christopher.
4. fable
5. The following should be underlined: "Cookie Monster Christopher, you better watch out. You eat too many cookies, and bad things happen to little boys who do that!" and "No more cookies for you today, Christopher. You should not eat more than one cookie per day!"
6. possible answers: He feels relieved not to be a cookie; grateful to eat a waffle for a change; glad nobody would try to eat him; certain he would never eat another cookie again.

Page 100
Answers will vary.

Page 101
1. be inactive
2. plant eater
3. alone
4. chew

Page 102
1. groundhog
2. weather
3. hibernate
4. winter
5. Germans
6. Candlemas

Page 103
1. He is a groundhog who predicts the weather every winter.
2. Gobbler's Knob; the town of Punxsutawney, Pennsylvania
3. "elixir of life"
4. a group of local dignitaries responsible for carrying on the tradition of Groundhog Day
5. Groundhogese
6. possible answers: Phil was able to meet President Ronald Reagan; he appeared on the *Oprah Winfrey Show*; in 2001, Phil's prediction was shown live on the JumboTron at Times Square in New York City.

Pages 104–105
1. The following should be underlined: "What do you mean, Mom? My math test was yesterday."
2. The following should be circled: Claire went to school, and all the day through, had the feeling that she had already seen and done the things that were happening to her. The problems on her math test looked really familiar, and she was certain the cafeteria had just had the identical lunch menu the day before.
3. Claire is reliving the day before—again!
4. The following should be underlined: She was utterly confused.
5. *I'm even having the same thoughts!*
6. The following should be underlined: Claire's mother had made spaghetti and meatballs for dinner the night before.
7. exactly the same as the other days
8. The following should be underlined: That's when Claire decided that if she were going to change her life back to normal, she'd have to shake things up.

Page 106
1. B
2. V
3. V
4. B
5. B

Page 107
1. Harvey Brooks
2. Cotton Club
3. more than 2,000
4. He hated them.
5. Washington, D.C.

Page 108
Answers will vary, but should reflect indicated parts of speech.

Page 109
1. eighth note
2. whole note
3. $\frac{1}{4}$ beat per measure
4. sixteenth note
5. whole note
6. A quarter note is filled in.

Page 110
1. January 8, 1935, in Tupelo, Mississippi
2. pop and country music of the time, gospel music in church, and R&B on historic Beale Street in Memphis, Tennessee
3. possible answers: Elvis appeared on many television shows and specials; he performed live concerts on tour and in Las Vegas; he sold more records than any other artist in the world—more than one billion records; he starred in 33 successful movies; he won three Grammy awards; he was awarded a Grammy Lifetime Achievement Award.
4. Graceland
5. The King of Rock 'n' Roll

Page 111
1. possible answers: She has stage fright; she is afraid to perform in front of a crowd at the Open Mic Night at camp.
2. She suggests that Charlotte picture the audience in their underwear.
3. possible answers: She might be scared again, but if she imagines the same thing, she'll be fine.
4. Answers will vary.

Page 112
1. c
2. a
3. b
4. a

Page 113
Stories will vary.

Pages 114–115
1. The staff has five lines and four spaces.
2. the pitch at any point during the music
3. all the notes between one letter and its next occurrence
4. a symbol that lets one know what octave to play the notes in, as well as what notes should be played.
5. A treble clef is used for higher musical voices, including soprano, mezzo-soprano, alto, and tenor.

It is also used for the higher-pitched musical instruments such as the alto clarinet, the B-Flat clarinet, the flute, the trumpet, and the oboe. By contrast, a bass clef is used for bass and baritone voices and lower-pitched musical instruments, such as the tuba, trombone, and sousaphone.
6. treble clef
7. Notes for the lower-pitched instruments would have to sit very low beneath the treble clef staff, making them hard for players to read. So the bass clef allows them to have a different staff that they can easily read.
8. possible answers: a word formed from the initial letters of each word in a phrase; an abbreviation

Page 116
1. possible answers: write, play, or listen to music
2. possible answers: proud, excited
3. possible answers: badly, like he might explode, hindered
4. possible answers: Mark will be successful at college, and surpass the other musicians there.
5. possible answers: be a composer, a music teacher, play music
6. possible answers: Adults might feel surprised that a child can play better than they can; adults might feel jealous.

Page 117
1. Juneau
2. Canada
3. Arctic
4. January 3, 1959
5. In terms of landmass, Alaska is the largest state.
6. Mt. McKinley

Pages 118–119
1. Answers will vary, but should include some of the following information: The Iditarod is an annual dogsled race in Alaska. The race is more than 1,150 miles long and follows a trail from Anchorage to Nome. The race starts on the first Saturday in March and takes about 10 days to complete. The winning dogsled racer wins a large cash prize.
2. Answers will vary, but should include some of the following information: The Iditarod dogsled race memorializes the "Great Race of Mercy," which was a real race against time that saved lives threatened by disease in the early part of the twentieth century. The Great Race of Mercy occurred in 1925, and it was certainly not a game or competition. In February

of that year, a diphtheria epidemic threatened the city of Nome, Alaska. Diptheria is a contagious and potentially fatal disease. Fortunately, diphtheria is rare in modern times, because children are vaccinated against it.

3. Answers will vary, but should include some of the following information: The lead dog of the final team to arrive in Nome was named Balto, a Siberian husky that has since become quite famous. There are statues of Balto in Anchorage and in Central Park, in New York City. There is even a movie about Balto, named after him. Sadly, Balto died on March 14, 1933, at the age of 14.

Page 120
1. true
2. false
3. false
4. false

Page 121
Drawing should resemble an Inuit, and may include a seal, igloo, dogsled, kayak, or anything else common to the Inuit people.

Pages 122–123
3 Make the base layer of the igloo by laying the blocks in a circle large enough to fit four or more people lying down.
8 For air circulation, cut one or two vents in the blocks.
4 The following row of blocks should be beveled at the bottom.
1 Start with a base area that you have stamped down with your feet.
7 Once you have reached the igloo chamber, dig up and into the igloo.
2 Have an adult help you cut blocks of snow and ice.
6 After the outer igloo is completed, dig an entrance through the ground approaching it. Dig down and over toward it.
5 Continue to work upward so that the height of the igloo is about as high as the shoulders of the person working inside.

Page 124
1. possible answer: July on a very hot day, in a city street
2. Jemma
3. possible answers: hot, then cool and wet
4. possible answer: her little brother Malcolm squealing with delight as he got wet.

Page 125
1. Japan
2. Mumbai
3. Japan
4. Philippines
5. 17,700,000
6. New York City

Pages 126–127
1. Higgins the dog
2. Higgins is lost in New York City.
3. possible answers: He doesn't know where to go; he's hungry and scared.
4. New York City and the places mentioned are real, but the talking animals and pigeons carrying a dog are fantasy.
5. possible answers: the squirrel, Clyde, Higgins's owner, the other pigeons
6. Higgins felt at home in his owner's arms, even if he was still far away from his country home.

Pages 128–129

Pages 130–131
1. Phineas Gage was a railroad foreman of a railway construction gang. The force of an accidental explosion drove a tamping iron rod into Gage's left cheekbone, through his skull, and out the top of his head.
2. possible answers: surprised, shocked, in disbelief
3. He had a huge hole in his head and his brain was exposed, but he was awake, alert, able to answer questions, sitting upright, and rational.
4. During the next few months, Phineas's personality underwent a dramatic shift. He became a completely different person.
5. possible answers: They began to understand that certain portions of the brain were responsible for different parts of personality; observing social convention, behaving ethically, and making good life choices required knowledge of strategies and rules that are separate from those necessary for basic memory, motor, and speech processing; there are systems in the brain dedicated primarily to reasoning.

Pages 132–133
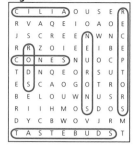

Page 134
1. femur; fibula
2. 206; 275
3. pelvis
4. tarsals; phalanges
5. phalanges

Page 135
1. secondary limbs for walking on all fours
2. due to ingestion of humans
3. sucking the brains out of captors
4. No one knows.
5. fantasy
6. possible answers: to entertain, to make the reader laugh

Page 136
Stories and drawings will vary.

Page 137
1. b
2. c
3. a
4. b
5. a
6. a

Page 138
1.
2.
3.
4.
5.
6.

Page 139
1. Hair sprouted from his ears.
2. fangs
3. His clothes felt tight because of the thick fur he's grown. This makes him feel hot, too, but he's not sweating. He's panting instead.
4. He has become a werewolf! He has fur and fangs, he pants instead of sweating, and he howls.

Page 140
1. shadow
2. tides
3. craters
4. meteors
5. life
6. rotation
7. cheese
8. man in the moon

Page 141
1. Jesse
2. Australia
3. Australia sits nearly at the "bottom" of the globe.
4. kangaroo
5. Kangaroos are marsupials. They are also sometimes killed for their meat. There's a lot of controversy about that in Australia.
6. possible answers: In Australia the people were more relaxed than in America; in Australia the pace was slower than in America.

Page 142
1. intricate
2. equidistant
3. temperate
4. blocking

Page 143
4 Swiftly and smoothly, bend your arm at the elbow, raising your hand with the rod until it reaches almost eye level.
6 Next, gently sweep the rod forward, causing the rod to bend with the motion.
7 As the rod moves in front of you and reaches an angle between 45° and 90° to your body, release your thumb from the button.
1 Face the target area with your body turned at a slight angle.
5 As the rod bends, move your forearm forward with a slight wrist movement.
3 Press and hold down the reel's release button.
2 Aim the rod tip toward the target, at about the level of your eyes.

possible answers: if you released the thumb button too late; if you released the thumb button too soon.

Page 144
Answers will vary, but should indicate the correct part of speech.

Page 145
1. fact
2. opinion
3. fact
4. fact
5. fact
6. opinion

Page 146
1. possible answers: ferocious, mean, scary
2. possible answers: Sammy seems friendly, but lonely. He doesn't have any friends.
3. possible answers: Marco is brave for approaching a great white shark, compassionate, helpful
4. The first problem is that his joke was not funny—the other sea creatures don't want to be eaten by him! The second problem is that his teeth are scary, for the same reason.
5. possible answer: Sammy

might change his approach to making friends. Marco will make him understand that he's scaring the other creatures.

Page 147
1. Zoey
2. Rome, Italy
3. Australia
4. possible answers: It's the seat of the Holy Roman Catholic Church and the home of the Pope; it's where Michelangelo painted the history of creation on the ceiling of the Sistine Chapel; it is the smallest state in the world.
5. possible answers: It was used as a church beginning in the early seventh century; the only light that enters the Pantheon comes from the opening at the dome's apex; it's where many famous Italians are buried, including the Renaissance painter Raphael.
6. good-bye

Page 148
5 Bake for 20 to 25 minutes, or until crust is brown.
3 Spread vegetables over sauce layer.
1 Preheat oven to 400°F.
4 Sprinkle cheese on top of vegetable layer.
2 Spread sauce over crust.

No, the recipe states that I can choose the variety of vegetables I prefer.

Page 149
1. peasants
2. Mediterranean ones, such as the Greeks, Egyptians, and Italians
3. Lombardi's in New York City
4. Spaniards
5. It was the type of pizza made by Raffaele Esposito that Queen Margherita apparently loved.

Page 150
1. diversity
2. Ancient Egypt
3. slaves
4. barren
5. colonized

Page 151
1. South Atlantic Ocean
2. Madagascar
3. South Africa
4. Sahara
5.

Page 152
1. possible answer:
Cape Town is backed by the flat-topped Table Mountain and nestled between the mountains and the sea. It has miles of pristine beaches and magnificent enclaves surrounded by oak trees.
2. European settlers who arrived in Cape Town in 1652
3. Kruger is Africa's oldest wildlife sanctuary, which stretches across 6.2 million acres.
4. The author saw many of the more than 500 bird and 147 mammal species, including lions, leopards, rhinos, and buffalo; San Bushman rock paintings; and elephants.
5. Cool!

Page 153
1. b
2. a
3. c
4. a

Pages 154–155
1. The following should be circled: pelican, pelted, penalties, penalizes
2. The following should be circled: massive, master, massage, massing, massed, massaged
3. The following should be circled: overjoyed, overloaded, overhead, overhearing, overlapped, overlapping
4. dog
5. noun
6. **a** : canine; *especially* : a domestic mammal (*Canis familiaris*) closely related to the gray wolf **b** : a male dog; *also* : a male usually carnivorous mammal
7. Any of the following: a worthless or contemptible person; fellow, chap; either of the constellations Canis Major or Canis Minor; feet; ruin

Page 156

Page 157
Answers will vary but could be: adorable, pretty; disobedient, mischievous; rations, fare, chow; garbage, rubbish, waste, litter; consumed, gobbled, munched, nibbled; terrible, awful, dreadful; vexed, concerned, troubled; scampered, jogged, sprinted; frolicked; wicked, impish

Pages 158–159
1. She liked to fish, play softball, swim, catch frogs, and ride around in hay wagons with her brothers.
2. After college, she was a reporter for the *Washington Post* newspaper and for the White House Press Corps.
3. *Vulpes, the Red Fox*
4. *Julie of the Wolves*
5. from a trip to Alaska in 1970 with her youngest child
6. possible answer: She loves animals, so she would probably take it in, care for it, or bring it to a proper animal shelter.

Page 160
1. He has been abandoned.
2. a shelter
3. a child and his parents who are there to adopt a dog
4. He has been adopted by the family and is in bed with the boy. He enjoys it very much.

Page 161
1. a
2. b
3. c
4. c

Page 162
1. a cat
2. the cat's owners
3. a bath
4. He thinks the dog is an accomplice and the bird is an informant.
5. by kneading them in bed and weaving between their feet
6. He dislikes it.

Page 163
1. Clive Staples (C.S.) Lewis
2. one at a time in the 1950s
3. Belfast, Ireland
4. the magical world of Narnia, where talking animals and kings, centaurs and dwarfs all exist
5. Later in his life he began to believe in Christianity and morality.
6. possible answers: They were so popular that Lewis received many letters from children who expressed their fascination with the world of Narnia. They are considered children's literary classics.

Page 164
1. The following should be circled: cornstarch, sugar, water, orange juice
2. Mix cornstarch with cold water and set aside. Roll in powdered sugar. Pour into buttered pan.

Page 165
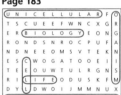

Page 166
1. true
2. true
3. false
4. false
5. true
6. true

Page 167
Answers will vary, but should indicate the correct part of speech.

Page 168
Stories will vary.

Page 169
1. pollution in the air and acid gases from factories, cars, and homes
2. possible answers: acid rain accelerates the decay of buildings; acid rain is damaging to the health of human beings, as water we drink from taps can be contaminated by acid rain, which can damage the brain; acid rain also has frightful effects on forests; fish and plants cannot survive in acidic lakes, so those lakes eventually "die."
3. People could use buses or trains instead of cars. People could buy hybrid cars.

Page 170
1. the atmosphere
2. The earth's surface absorbs and warms it.
3. The rest is reflected by the earth and atmosphere.
4. infrared radiation
5. Some of it passes back out through the atmosphere. Some of it is absorbed by gas molecules.
6. It warms the atmosphere.

Page 171
1. The Simpsons
2. cartoon
3. Matt Groening
4. Emmy
5. Bart
6. Homer

Pages 172–173
1. Michelangelo painted it because the Pope commissioned him to paint it.
2. The Sistine Chapel is the chapel in the Apostolic Palace, which is the official residence of the Pope.
3. possible answers: Michelangelo had to lie on his back to paint it; he had to make a scaffold to paint it; it took him four years of work; the Pope was slow to pay him; mold; the Pope was closely watching the painting as it was done.
4. possible answers: He is famous for doing so; his vision was damaged.
5. possible answer: honored
6. possible answers: dedicated; talented; visionary
7. possible answers: He did much more than he was asked to do; he spent four years of his life doing it, despite obstacles.

Page 174
1. a
2. c
3. b
4. c

Page 175
1. fact
2. fact
3. opinion
4. fact
5. opinion

Page 176
Drawings and explanations will vary.

Page 177
Answers and drawings will vary, but the drawing should reflect the written answers.

Pages 178–179
1. F
2. N
3. F
4. N
5. N
6. F
7. N
8. N

Pages 180–181
1. ugly, unwanted, unloved
2. No, his mother and siblings should have loved him, anyway.
3. possible answers: This was because he was different and people do not like things that are different; they often perceive them as unattractive, wrong, or bad.
4. a kind farmer
5. He is cared for through the winter. He grows large and healthy.
6. possible answers: He is relieved that others think he is beautiful and that he finally found his own kind; he is happy and excited.

Page 182
1. He thought a trick was being played on him.
2. It was made of solid gold.
3. He was poor and knew he could sell the egg for money.
4. He became greedy, and so to get all the eggs immediately, he killed the goose, and there were no more eggs inside it.
5. possible answer: Greed is destructive.

Page 183
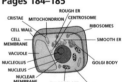

Pages 184–185
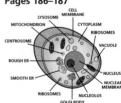

Pages 186–187